Nail every performance!

Theresa

ALSO BY THERESA ROSE

Opening the Kimono:
A Woman's Intimate Journey Through Life's Biggest Challenges
(Out of print)

Start Now, Grow Big

Bits of Bigness:
Inspirational Nuggets to Remind You of Your Magnificence

Your Daily Dose of Mojo:
365 Days of Mindful Living and Working

MINDFUL
PERFORMANCE

....

How to
POWERFULLY IMPACT
PROFITABILITY,
PRODUCTIVITY,
& PURPOSE

THERESA ROSE

Printed in the United States of America
First Printing 2018
ISBN-13: 978-0-9818869-5-4

Serious Mojo Publications
Minneapolis, MN
TheresaRose.com

Bulk discounts available.

DEDICATION

For Prince Rogers Nelson
A creative genius and Minnesota performance legend

....

*"To make this cruel, cruel world hear what we've got to say,
put the right letters together and make a better day."*

ALPHABET ST.

TABLE OF CONTENTS

·

CHAPTER 1

INTRODUCTION

....

Congratulations! You have made the bold decision to live and work intentionally. I am thrilled to be going on the journey with you to create a more successful career and a richer, more meaningful life. Consider this book your how-to field guide into a world I call *Mindful Performance*. Contained within these pages are dozens of proven business strategies, success tools, and powerful nuggets of inspiration that will help you reverse the harmful effects of an unbalanced, overwhelmed life and unleash your fullest potential both professionally and personally. **With mindful performance, you can and will make more time, get more done, earn more money, and have more fun.** Is there anyone among us who wouldn't want (and need) more of those?

In a nutshell, you will get more of what you want and less of what you don't. Many of us now have less of what we need: fewer resources at work (while having more to do than ever before), less money to pay for college education, costly medical bills or retirement funds, and worst of all, less quality time spent with the people we love, doing what is truly important to us.

Life is getting more complicated by the minute, and stress levels are at an all-time high. You can see it in people's faces and in the ways they conduct themselves. Most are either angry or have their heads buried in their phones. It is becoming increasingly rare to find people who actually enjoy their lives and create the success they desire. Many are too busy with shiny objects and self-medication to notice that life is passing them by. According to the American Psychological Association, 75% of adults have experienced moderate to high levels of stress in the past month and nearly half reported that their stress has increased in the past year.[1] The American Institute of Stress reports that 80% of workers feel stress on the job, and nearly half of the workforce says they need help learning how to manage stress.[2] People are reaching for bottles, pills, processed foods, and electronic devices in an attempt to quell the pain of living in an overstressed, distracted and increasingly frightening, fragmented world. Life expectancy is actually lower than it has been in decades. *People are literally dying from the stress.*

Based on my experience as an organizational consultant, professional speaker, and personal development expert, I believe the answers to our most pressing issues are found in the practices of mindfulness and mental mastery. Mindfulness itself is a relatively simple concept to understand—**being fully aware of the present moment and choosing intentionally**—but is quite challenging for most of us to actually execute on a daily basis. Dr. Jon Kabat-Zinn, the founding Executive Director of the Center for Mindfulness in Medicine at the University of Massachusetts Medical School, is widely considered to be the father of modern mindfulness studies. His revolutionary program, Mindfulness-Based Stress Reduction (MBSR), is the standard-bearer for mindfulness training and has been implemented in organizations all over the world for years. Dr. Kabat-Zinn's definition of mindfulness is "paying attention in a particular way: on purpose, in the present moment, and nonjudgmentally".[3] This definition is brilliant in its simple clarity and serves as the backdrop for all the strategies contained in "Mindful Performance".

My goal is to make mindfulness and its relationship to performance as easy to absorb and implement as possible. These practices aren't for a select few; they are for all of us (even those of us who are highly stressed). It involves demonstrating awareness, focus, and conscious choice in a variety of challenging scenarios and uncontrolled environments that we all face each day. It's about being aware and accountable without judging yourself or others and taking conscious action toward a richer, more meaningful life for yourself and those around you. We perform better in the human race when we practice these techniques on a regular basis.

There is growing evidence emerging every day that highlights the critical correlation between our thoughts and our physical realities. One only needs to Google "Mindfulness Scientific Research" to uncover hundreds of rigorous studies across a variety of environments which have definitively demonstrated the profound impact our minds have on our desired outcomes. High performance athletes utilize it. Inspiring leaders utilize it. Sales ninjas utilize it. Great thinkers utilize it. Educators utilize it. Soldiers utilize it. Children utilize it.

Mindfulness can have a transformational impact on every single person who chooses to take up the practice. Consider the below examples:

- Elite athlete Michael Jordan used mindfulness training under the brilliant leadership of Phil Jackson to win six NBA championship rings with my beloved Chicago Bulls.

- Innovative juggernaut Steve Jobs used meditation practices to quiet his mind prior to his highest-stakes product launch presentations.

- Genius Albert Einstein regularly sat in quiet solitude before discovering some of his greatest theories.

- A military veteran with PTSD uses mind-body medicine to treat his debilitating pain.

- Antsy elementary school students use sitting still to address their behavioral issues.

Thankfully, the science of neuroplasticity—the brain's ability to reorganize itself by forming new neural pathways throughout our lives—shows us it is never too late to make substantive improvements in our brain chemistry, and thus our life experiences. When you couple the theories of mindfulness with proven strategies of high performance management, a powerful framework is formed that can and will create the kind of success you dream about. In my humble opinion, **you are holding in your hands the answers to every critical need you have in every area of your life: physical, mental, emotional, spiritual, financial, vocational, relational, and recreational.** Pretty exciting!

If you are like me, your first question may be, "So why should I listen to what this person has to say? What makes her so knowledgeable?" Here's a bit more about my background so you can be confident that I know what I'm talking about. I began my professional career as a temp and administrative professional (back in those days I was called a secretary). Thanks to the early teachings from my powerhouse single mother/direct sales superstar, I have always felt confident tackling new opportunities and challenging scenarios. I could get projects done quickly and effectively, approaching them as puzzles to be solved. By combining my affinity for problem-solving with an authentic, energetic demeanor (I was named "Most Enthusiastic" by Mr. Moseman, my second-grade teacher), I rapidly grew as a professional. This resulted in my holding increasingly challenging positions in leadership, project management, and consulting. In my last corporate role, I was in senior management in Marketing and Product Development for a Fortune 100 company, directly responsible for more than a hundred million dollars of annual revenue. I was making more money and quickly moving up the ladder. Then in 2003, my life had what I call the first of many "snow globe moments"—you know those moments when life swirls you around, flips you upside down, and you don't have a clue which end is up.

Because of a company-wide reduction in force, I found myself job hunting and finding no success. Instead of landing another traditional management role in Corporate America, I took a 180 degree turn into a career in mind-body medicine. (I always had an affinity for intuitive studies, creative visualization, and complementary and alternative medicine, so it wasn't entirely outside my wheelhouse.) Over the next several years, I attended massage therapy school and expanded my understanding of energy medicine, states of consciousness, and mental training. I owned an alternative healing center in Sarasota, Florida where I performed healing and coaching sessions for individuals struggling with a variety of physical, mental and emotional ailments. In addition to my private practice, I became a Reiki Master and Approved Provider from the Nationally Certified Board of Therapeutic Massage and Bodywork, conducted weekly yoga and meditation classes, and facilitated deep-dive personal development retreats. In addition to my work in the healing center, I was a contributing columnist for a health magazine and a local newspaper, focusing on how one can use practical, proven mindfulness techniques to deal with the stressors we face every day. Since I was part hippie and part hardcore businesswoman, I was able to blend the esoteric with the practical, helping people to actually improve their lives through presence and conscious action.

What I discovered—and continue to discover—is that mindfulness expertise does not come solely from reading books, attending lectures, or earning certificates. Its true power lies in the practice itself. In my studies of mindfulness, I have participated in a breadth and depth of experiential learning from masters in the field of mind-body medicine. Whether it was in a classroom, at a meditation circle, in a sweat lodge, on a mountaintop, at sacred sites, or simply on my yoga mat, I have clocked thousands of hours exploring my inner landscape, allowing me to embody the mindfulness teachings you will learn in this powerful how-to book.

You will discover how to make your life healthier, more meaningful, more abundant, and just plain easier.

Don't worry if you are a newbie to mindfulness. In fact, being a beginner (or having a beginner's mind) is an ideal place to start on the path of mindful performance. It's perfectly fine if you have never had one drop of exposure to meditation, visualization, purposeful breathwork, or mental toughness training. Whether you are brand new or a seasoned mindfulness practitioner, I guarantee **you will learn memorable, highly-effective, actionable strategies that will unlock your true potential** and make life more abundant than you can possibly imagine.

Just imagine creating a life where you ...

- **Make more time** for yourself, your relationships, and your passions

- **Get more done at work**, at home, and within the community

- **Earn more money** as a leader and salesperson (we all are)

- **Have more fun** to truly relish life instead of merely enduring it

"Mindful Performance" will show you how to leverage the massive power you possess in the six inches between your ears. You will receive the essence of critical mind training so you can stop paying partial attention and start being fully present. You'll hone your ability to focus on the important work while letting go of the noise and distraction that are keeping your stress levels higher than they need to be.

So, let's practice a bit. I invite you to perform the imagination exercise I just described, but this time with a little more thoughtful awareness brought to it. In the bullet points above, I gave you some starting points for creative visualization, using your mind to mentally create your circumstances before they come to fruition in the *physical state*.

As you perform the exercise again, take a few moments to settle into your chair a little deeper. Shrug your shoulders a few times and do some neck rolls to release any excess physical tension. Take several big, deep, cleansing breaths, maybe even make a sound as you exhale out any tension. Really settle into your body and notice any sensations. Give yourself permission to spend at least one minute visualizing every one of the bullet points. Fill in the details—the people, the places, and the activities that would be involved. Pay particular attention to how the thought of accomplishing each of those particular objectives *feels*. Eliciting the feeling state, or what is referred to as kinesthetic visualization, is critical in order to maximize the effect. Allow your life movie to play out in your mind's eye exactly how you wish it to be.

Now let's read those again, but this time with a mindful approach, spending at least a minute visualizing each bullet point:

Imagine, *really imagine*, what it will feel like to:

- **Have more time** for yourself, your relationships, and your passions.

   (Go ahead and imagine it!)

- **Get more done** at work, at home, and within the community.

   (What specific projects would you complete?)

- **Earn more money** as a leader and salesperson (we all are).

   (How much more money? What is the number?)

- **Have more fun** to truly relish life instead of merely enduring it.

   (What activities would you love to be doing right now?)

How different did the exercise feel after making conscious adjustments to your breath and body, giving you more time to be fully present and savoring each example instead of rushing through them? Slowing down and really thinking about it made it more vivid, right? Hopefully the exercise elicited some positive, expansive, and motivating feelings.

That's the goal of mindful performance: to consciously create a feeling state of success, contentment, and empowerment in order to bring about your desired reality.

I promise that when you embrace the teachings and strategies contained in "Mindful Performance", you will intentionally create all of these scenarios and so much more. You will possess a mindset of growth and contentment that will permeate all you do at work, at home, and in your community from this point forward. People will be attracted to you. Time will slow down. You will be able to intentionally move into what positive psychologists call "the flow state", the optimal state of consciousness where we perform at our best and feel our best. Sounds great, right?

Yes, mindful performance really is that amazing! By reading and taking action on the strategies in this book, you will intentionally create a life and a career that are more profitable, productive, and purposeful.

Are you ready to ditch the stress and take back control of your health, your career, your schedule, and your relationships? Let's do this!

CHAPTER 2

THE MINDFUL
PERFORMANCE MODEL

....

As part of my thought leadership in the study of mindful performance, I am committed to helping you absorb the transformational concepts and strategies in the simplest yet most impactful way possible. I created the Mindful Performance Model and an easy-to-digest Mindful Performance Matrix to increase your understanding, application, and integration of my teachings. The model addresses nine major areas of focus that individuals and organizations can utilize to improve their outcomes and up-level their experiences on a daily basis. Let's take a tour of the model so you get a picture of the journey we are going to take together.

First, you'll notice that mindfulness is in the center, touching every single focus area. Mindfulness is ground zero, your touchstone, the place where all improvement begins.

Your awareness, your presence, and your mindful choices are at the hub of all you do in every area of your life.

Second, there are nine key focus areas of growth and potentiality that have the biggest influence on your ability to improve your performance:

- Movement
- Meditations
- Manifestations
- Meetings
- Mentors & Masterminds
- Messages
- Media
- Messes
- Meals & ZZZZs

Chapters 3-11 explain each of these areas. They address your body/mind health, your communications with others, and your environments.

Third, you'll notice three time segments on the model: At Home, At Work, and All Day. These segments are not affixed to any particular focus area but rather are designed to rotate around the model, touching all nine at any given time. After all, it isn't enough to be mindful solely at work or at home. To make exponential improvement and truly ramp up your performance while attaining a consistent state of balance, you'll need to adopt a constant vigilant posture at any time, in any environment. **Mindful living is not a part-time gig.**

"Mindful Performance" uses this intuitive, comprehensive, and dynamic model as your roadmap for getting more of what you want, walking you through how to leverage and optimize mindfulness in the nine key areas of your growth and potentiality in a variety of circumstances and locations. Every chapter explores one key focus area and has three sections—At Home, At Work, All Day—where you will find specific strategies or mindsets you can use to improve the quality, efficiency, and output of each area.

At the end of the book I have included a Mindful Performance Matrix which summarizes all 81 recommendations in one handy location. However, I've made it even easier for you by creating a handful of SuperStrategies. (These are my tried-and-true go-to activities that should be in everyone's mindfulness toolkit.) Committing them to memory and utilizing them regularly will serve you well professionally and personally for years to come.

As you read "Mindful Performance", jot down, highlight, or dog-ear the pages that contain the most impactful strategies that you *will* employ, and keep the book close at hand to remind you to take purposeful action every single day. It's a perfect bedside read to start and end each day with presence-centered awareness. Once you have digested the book in its entirety, you may want to regularly refer to the Mindful Performance Model and the Mindful Performance Matrix to remind you of the specific actions you can take to address your current challenges, whether they pertain to work, health, home, relationships, or any other major aspect of your life. If you bought the book, you can even rip those pages out and post them somewhere where you can easily refer to them every day.

The tools you are about to receive won't just help you live a more balanced life, they will also help you improve the results you deliver in the workplace. As an organizational consultant, I have seen how using the strategies in "Mindful Performance" can transform corporate cultures and their teams to not only become more aware of their behaviors and their consequences, but also to increase their personal presence so they can improve their results and positively impact the bottom line. Employees learn effective techniques they can use to address conflict, foster higher levels of performance, and consciously turn off damaging stress triggers. They discover how to build stronger connections and collaborations with their key influencers and customers. By consciously choosing thoughts, language, and specific actions that support each of the key areas in the Mindful Performance Model, you and your organization will deliver optimal productivity that leads to optimal success. This isn't wishful thinking; it's real-world practicality.

Allow me to tell you about one company in particular that has made mindfulness a core aspect of its culture. Mark Bertolini is the CEO of Aetna, a Fortune 100 insurance company with more than $30 billion in annual revenue. Mr. Bertolini had a personal health crisis after a horrifying ski accident several years ago and eventually turned to mindfulness training and yoga to address his debilitating pain. He realized that it also helped him to reduce his stress and make better decisions. (Mindfulness has been proven to positively impact the executive control functions of the frontal lobe of the brain such as planning, analysis, discernment, and decision-making.)

Mr. Bertolini knew his company would benefit from having his workforce receive mindfulness training. As a result, he authorized a twelve-week study whereby almost 250 of his most stressed employees would learn simple techniques to quiet their minds and reduce their stress. Compared to the control group, the participants who learned mindfulness reported a significant reduction in stress and improved sleep. This resulted in healthcare savings of $2,000 per employee and more than an hour per week gained in productivity, which amounted to $3,000 per employee. The organization's total healthcare costs fell 7%, with $6.3 billion going directly to the bottom line. The bonus: Happier, more fulfilled, more focused, and more loyal employees. Aetna now has a Chief Mindfulness Officer who oversees the entire program.[4]

The concepts contained in this book are bottom-line, hardcore smart business practices.

In order to effect substantive, permanent improvements in your professional and personal life, new neural pathways must be created and new long-lasting habits must be established. Reading through "Mindful Performance" one time and putting it on the shelf will not generate exponential growth. However, if you incorporate this book's concepts into your daily life, you will find that the answers you seek to nearly any challenge or upset are contained in these pages and within you. In addition, if you find yourself struggling in any specific area down the line (e.g. sleep, meetings, media, meditations, and so on) you can always revisit those sections to nudge yourself in the right direction and get the mental juices flowing again. **At its core, "Mindful Performance" is about YOU: your success at work, at home, in relationships, in community, and within. By utilizing its resources and strategies, you will get in the driver's seat of your own experience so you can consciously create the healthy, abundant, and satisfying life you desire.**

Now that we know the framework from which we will operate, let's get into the meat of the model and tackle the first key area of growth and potentiality: movement.

CHAPTER 3

MOVEMENT

....

One of my favorite childhood memories is when my older brothers and I would take our annual road trips with Gram and Gramp. Gram's job was to provide plenty of snacks and games, and Gramp's role was to make sure that their trusty Oldsmobile (he called it a "jalopy") was in the proper condition to transport his precious cargo. He made sure the oil was changed, air was in the tires, washer fluid was topped off, and quality fuel was in the gas tank. He even washed it so we wouldn't depart in a filthy car.

Gramp wanted to avoid any possible problems down the road. Once the jalopy was ready, we were on our way; for a week every summer, we would enjoy the beautiful Midwest countryside and (mostly) each other's company. With no phones or technology to waste away the time, Gram would provide the entertainment with her handmade Mad Libs she'd write in her steno notebook. That's all we needed to make it an adventure that we would remember for a lifetime.

Gramp taught me that every trip worth taking started with a vehicle that was in tip-top shape. This same principle holds true with our own journey to intentionally impact our profitability, productivity, and purpose. Our bodies are the one vehicle we have been given. We pay a price when we ignore the basic-but-necessary maintenance of our bodies (nutrition, sleep, and exercise, to name but a few).

When I started to integrate the teachings of mindful eating and movement several years ago, I realized how truly important vehicle maintenance is. We'll be talking about the quality of our fuel in Chapter 11, but right now let's dive into the topic of movement as a core aspect of our success.

The healthier, more flexible, and stronger our bodies are, the further we can take them. Have you ever thought about starting a new project or following up on a dormant one, only to convince yourself that you simply don't have the energy to complete it? It's not that you aren't talented enough, smart enough, or determined enough; it's that your vehicle just doesn't have the oomph needed to get you there. In order to get your vehicle on the road to greater productivity and success, the first step is to include some form of exercise every day. Yes, every day.

AT HOME

I'm a firm believer in eliminating excuses that prohibit us from taking action. As a result, I recommend that at least some of your daily movement happen at home. Without the need for a costly gym membership, a certified instructor, or fancy equipment, you can have an effective exercise regimen without ever leaving your house.

MOVE RIGHT AWAY

How many times have you thought to yourself, "I *really* need to exercise. My doctor has lectured me about it, and I not only want to look better but feel better. I'll promise to do it when I get home from work." Permit me to be dubious. By the time you return home, you are likely exhausted from a taxing day at work as well as all the other obligations on your shoulders. Exercising at the end of a long day is about as inviting as an icy shower.

The truth is, if we don't do some form of movement right away upon waking, we often won't get to it at all. Despite our best intentions, our days slip away from us and we simply don't have the energy to move our bodies after a hard day at work. Inactive days become weeks, which turn into inactive lives.

According to the Centers for Disease Control and Prevention, every year an estimated 300,000 U.S. deaths occur because of physical inactivity and poor eating habits, and 25% of adults report zero non-leisure physical activity.[5] An inactive lifestyle contributes to greater stress, anxiety, low self-esteem, obesity, high blood pressure, diabetes, heart disease, and stroke. None of these disorders and diseases help us make more time, get more done, earn more money, and have more fun.

Consider incorporating some form of movement beyond walking from the bed to the bathroom to the kitchen to the car. If you are lucky enough to live in a climate where you can go outside, that's even better. The fresh air will perk you up and supercharge you for the day ahead.

There was a wonderful paper written in 2008 in *Psychological Science* that studied the effect exposure to nature can have on our ability to concentrate. According to the research, the group who walked on a wooded path versus those who walked a busy city street performed up to 20% better on concentration tests.[6] It's worth getting a breath of fresh air every day!

Just as you would likely never start a morning without your beloved java or tea, consider movement in the same way. It is a core ingredient in your quest for higher performance levels, jump starting your day and planting you on firm ground instead of on your heels.

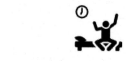

MORNING MOMENTUM

If you want to set your entire day in motion in a powerful, energizing, and positive way, start by implementing a Morning Momentum regimen that incorporates strategies found in the Movement, Meditations, and Manifestations chapters. It's the quickest way to ensure you will live your day intentionally and with ample energy to accomplish your objectives. Take one strategy from each section and perform them as soon as possible upon waking up. Don't get on your phone or social media. Don't mindlessly get ready for work. Don't start other tasks that will pull you away from your state of presence. The mornings are wonderful opportunities for you to catalyze your mindful performance practice.

An effective Morning Momentum routine should be enjoy-able, easy to remember, and accommodate any environment. The actions you take don't need to take a lot of time. In fact, the keys to establishing a consistent Morning Momentum routine are *simplicity* and *swiftness*. No more than 10 to 30 minutes are required to get your body moving, your mind quiet, and your vision attuned to your goals. If it takes too long, you won't do it. It's better to have a brief Morning Momentum practice that you will actually do each day than have an elaborate, lengthy process that is unrealistic.

My personal Morning Momentum practice involves a series of three, 10-minute sessions. The first 10 minutes are performed on my yoga mat where I do several forward bends, spinal twists, neck rolls, and any other stretch my body is calling for. The second 10 minutes are dedicated to sitting on my meditation pillow in silence and simply noticing my breath. The third 10-minute session involves a detailed exploration of my vision and the corresponding feeling state it elicits. In the subsequent chapters on Meditations and Manifestations, you will learn exactly how to perform these second and third sessions.

By executing a Morning Momentum every morning, you will be invigorating your body with vibrant energy, establishing a baseline of focus for your day, and cultivating an ongoing awareness of your life vision so it may become a reality.

MOVEMENT TOOLKIT

When you install a curtain rod, you need a measuring tape to measure the window for an accurate hardware placement, a pencil to mark the spots on the wall, a ladder to climb to create the right leverage, and an electric drill to install the hardware itself. Without any of these tools readily available, the job becomes far more difficult. (I should know; I've tried and dismally failed in the past.)

The same is true about your movement practice. What tools do you need in your Movement Toolkit to be successful? I will outline some of the exercise tools and equipment I recommend you use. I encourage you not to see the purchase of these items as extravagant excesses; they are, in fact, critical ingredients to your optimal productivity and should be readily accessible. In the interest of having an HGTV decorator-approved home, we often hide the more practical, mundane aspects of healthy living, including our exercise equipment and accessories. However, when we hide them, we forget about them. ("Out of sight, out of mind" is a timeless adage for a reason; it's *true*.)

When we tuck our tools nicely away in our closets, basement, or garage, we've added a barrier to use that keeps us from establishing long-term habits.

Let's be real; who in their right mind is going to dig out all the equipment they need every morning or go down to the unfinished basement to use the treadmill?

Below are some of the tools in my Movement Toolkit that help me to move my body as consistently as possible. Hopefully they will inspire you to get your own tools that will support your daily movement goals.

- **Proper workout togs.** Having the right exercise apparel is critical. Whether it's yoga pants and top, track suit, dance slippers, or running shoes, invest in quality clothes that allow you to move your body with comfort and freedom. I shop consignment stores all the time for work outfits and fancy frocks, but I will not cut corners when it comes to my workout gear. If you don't have the clothes and shoes, you won't do it. Get them. Right now.

- **MP3 player with Bluetooth speaker or headphones.** Our favorite tunes provide the soundtrack to our lives. Don't forget to bring these musical gems into your movement practice. It's amazing how much motivation the right toe-tapping song will give us. Create a playlist that includes all your favorites that will get your blood pumping and mood elevated.

- **Yoga mat.** I think every single human should have a mat upon which to stretch. Even if you don't know your asana from a hole in the ground, you still can get on that sucker and do some twists, bends, stretches, and folds. Nobody wants to lay on scratchy carpet or hard floors. If you are planning on doing any balance work at all, you absolutely need a yoga mat to maintain a solid foundation. (Bare feet only! No socks or shoes.) By the way, the greatest risk of injury for older adults is falls, so establishing a yoga routine that includes balance postures will keep you safer as you age and reduce costly medical bills resulting from a nasty slip on the ice. Don't buy a big thick workout mat that we used as kids in tumbling class. A yoga mat that you would see at a professional studio is the kind you need.

- **Acu-ball.** I use this little ball of torture on the bottoms of my feet to give myself my own reflexology treatment, stimulating the nerve endings which can contribute to leg and back issues if left untreated. It also helps treat plantar fasciitis, which is a common ailment for those who log a lot of foot-time. (I was a bartender for a while and standing for long periods of time wreaked havoc on my lower back—as any nurse, server, hairdresser, or clerk can attest.) For me, the more my Acu-ball hurts, the better it is. If you aren't making guttural, not-of-this-earth sounds when rolling on your ball, you aren't going deep enough.

- **Foam Roller and Lacrosse Ball.** Our muscles and connective tissue need to be massaged regularly, otherwise they create adhesions and become stiff and painful. Short of receiving a professional, deep-tissue massage every single week, we need to figure out how to treat ourselves on an ongoing basis. (If you've got the resources, I highly recommend receiving professional bodywork regularly. It's worth it.) Enter the instruments of torture known as self-massage myofascial release tools. These are designed to get into the deepest part of your muscular system known as the fascia, the interconnected web of tissue that surrounds every single muscle. Roll s...l...o...w...l...y on these devices (or better yet, park it on a particularly needful spot) to give yourself a deep-tissue massage that may not feel like one you'd get in a spa, but definitely one that will help you perform better. It will improve your flexibility, address areas of pain, and decrease your stress.

- **Elastic bands.** I personally have no interest in being super ripped (nor do I think I could feasibly do so at my age and childbirth history), but I do want to avoid wizard-wings as much as possible. I use long elastic bands to work out my biceps, triceps, and lats. It's an easy way to log some muscle toning exercises without having to have a bunch of dumbbells around.

- **Core trainer.** This is my newest toy, and I love her. It is a peanut-shaped, nubby, inflatable tool that allows me to work on my core strength, enabling me to improve my posture and address my lower back pain. While constantly squeezing it, I slowly move it up, down and side-to-side, engaging my core muscles the entire time. It also is the perfect little pillow for my sacrum (the trian-gular bone right at the base of the spine) to stretch out that tired sacroiliac joint. I watched the tutorial a few times before I got the routine, and now it's a part of every morning.

What will be included in your Movement Toolkit, and where will it be located for easy access and usage? Don't put off the process of getting what you need to be healthy. Do it now.

AT WORK

....

Contrary to what we may occasionally tell ourselves, work is not a mere inconvenience nestled between "real life" moments; it is an essential part of our experience, one that occupies much of our waking time. Being mindful of how we move at work is just as important as how we move at home.

Here are a few strategies that will help you fight off workplace stress, improve your health, and generally make you a more pleasant person to be around, all of which will help you when motivating your team members, making that next business call, or going for the promotion you've been eyeing forever.

RISE AT THE ZEROES

It's easy to plop ourselves down at work and grow roots on our office chairs for hours. When we do so, we are not only doing a disservice to our bodies, but we are also robbing our brains of some much-needed oxygen which helps us keep our creative edge and allows us to be more attentive listeners. The best way to establish good work movement habits is to set up a memory device that will help trigger you to take action. Consider getting up from your desk every hour on the hour (if you won't remember, set an alarm on your phone) to look up, stretch your body, and walk around a few moments. You don't have to make it a big deal; just create a habit of getting off your chair for a few minutes at the top of every hour.

Whether it's to refill your water bottle, go to the restroom, or do some chair yoga, get up and move several times throughout the day. Even if you just push your chair away from your desk for a few moments to do some neck and shoulder rolls with deep breathing, you will refresh and revitalize your energy. Your body will thank you, and your level of creativity and productivity will skyrocket.

SMART INEFFICIENCY

We live in a hyper-efficient world. Why go to three stores to pick up your groceries, household items, and updates to your wardrobe when you can just go online and order from the comfort of your own bed? We have been trained to manically manage our time down to the minute in the elusive quest to create extra moments of "spare" time. As a mindful performance expert, I am all for utilizing time as smartly and efficiently as possible. However, sometimes it serves us better if we are a little less efficient, especially at work.

Where can you add a few extra steps during your workday?

- Can you park your car at the far end of the parking lot?

- Can you visit your colleagues at their office instead of emailing them?

- Can you walk down to the mailroom instead of dropping it in your outbox to be picked up?

- Can you use the bathroom located on the other side of the office one time each day?

- Can you go to the central printer station instead of fighting to have one located on your desk?

- Can you take a walk at lunchtime?

There are steps waiting to be had if we look closely enough. Those extra moments will keep you refreshed, flexible, and better able to focus on the task at hand when you return to your workspace. Go ahead. Spend those few extra minutes; they will ultimately help you create a movement-oriented mindset. When you do take advantage of those inefficiencies, don't lollygag to your destination; this isn't an excuse to disengage. Go forth with gusto! But just remember, this isn't a break; it's mobile work.

SQUEEZE AND RELEASE

Do you ever have muscle tension that interferes with your ability to concentrate at work? Most of us hold our stress somewhere in our bodies. Mine tends to go to my neck and shoulder area, particularly in my ill-behaved trapezius muscles. If you want to check to see if that area bothers you as well, take your right hand (or left if you are a leftie like me) and grab a big chunk of muscle between your neck and shoulder. Squeeze that big ropey muscle as hard as you can between your thumb and fingers. Is it soft and easily pliable, or does it feel like a steel bar? (If you are like me, it's the latter.) Give it a few more squeezes and then release your hand, allowing the muscle to relax. Doesn't that feel better? Now do the other side, just to make sure you are balanced on both sides.

Your stress center may be located in the neck area or lower back. Or maybe it's in your face. Or arms. Or legs. You get the idea. When we are in any position for extended periods of time, our muscles tend to lock up. Add a dash of anxiety and annoyance, and our bodies *really* take a beating. But we can mindfully choose to reverse work stress and strain by using Progressive Muscle Relaxation, or what I like to call the Squeeze and Release strategy.

Imagine you could feel better literally from head to toe, every day.

- You would show up stronger and more confident for that big important meeting.

- You would be more creative.

- You would have more endurance.

- You would be fully present at the tail end of the workday.

The Squeeze and Release technique is your way to subtly self-administer a powerful muscle relaxant/stress regulator. This strategy will give you not only a competitive edge, but it will also keep you operating in the flow state as long as possible.

Squeeze and Release is an elegant exercise that treats our physical, mental, and emotional bodies.

By bringing our awareness to each part of our bodies from head to toe, we instantly become present.

Honing our body awareness helps improve our ability to focus and gives us a tangible sensation to which to bring our attention. It's mindfulness in action.

Start by puckering your face like you just ate the sourest lemon. Squeeze every facial feature—your eyes, your nose, your mouth, your chin, your cheeks, and even your ears. As you squeeze, acknowledge all the stress, worry, doubt, or anger you might be feeling in that moment. Squeeze your face! And then release it with a big, cleansing exhalation, letting go of the physical tension, the mental chatter, and the negative emotions.

Next, move to the shoulders. Squeeze them way up to your ears, again acknowledging any unpleasant or worrisome feelings that you may be feeling. Hold it for a few seconds and then release.

Do this for the entire body—the arms, the hands and fingers, the torso and back, the legs, and even the feet and toes. Squeeze each, acknowledge your emotions, and release. After just a few minutes performing this exercise from head to toe, your body will feel less tense and more flexible, your mind will also be sharper, and your emotions will be better regulated. Progressive Muscle Relaxation exercises are used in yoga classes, in schoolrooms, and even in the military. Members of the armed services who learn mindfulness techniques and mind/body medicine rely on this powerful technique to manage their pain and regulate their stress. It is a wonderful tool for you to use every day as you combat your constant stressors.

ALL DAY

Mindful movement is a lifestyle choice, one that invites extra steps and increased expenditure of energy at every turn. If using a Fitbit helps to remind you to move, then go for it! My daughter bought me one a few years ago. While I appreciated the sentiment, I didn't need a $100 bracelet to remind me that I needed to lose weight; I had jeans for that.

Let's look at some simple ways you can incorporate more movement every day so you can take care of your precious body inside and out.

JOYFUL MOVEMENT

I loathe the word "exercise". It reminds me too much of the word "exorcise", which calls forth images of a very unhappy girl named Regan in "The Exorcist." Exercise is filled with requirements, judgment, obligation, and must-do's. (We talk in terms of repetitions, working up a sweat, calories burned, core muscle activation—that sounds awful.) No wonder many people are reluctant to exercise.

My relationship with my body changed when I finally found a form of movement that I actually loved doing—hoop dancing. Prior to waking up to the power of the hoop and more importantly, giving myself permission to dance, I avoided movement like the plague. Just like getting out of running the mile, I was the kid who found creative reasons to get excused from the swimming module. I would rather have had a fork to the eye than do anything resembling aerobic activity.

When I was growing up, I loved TV shows and movies about dancing. You could say I have a dancer's soul. But I didn't have a dancer's body, so I never gave myself permission to follow my passion. That is, until hoop dancing entered my life. Hoop dancing combines hula hooping with dance, and it is the most fun people can have with their clothes on. I finally found something that stirred my soul! Because of that love, I made time to do it for many years, even if it was five o'clock in the morning at the YMCA open gym. As a result, I lost fifty pounds and more importantly, kept them off. We make time for things we love, no matter how busy we are.

However, sometimes it isn't convenient or appropriate for us to perform our favorite activity. Whether it's an injury that keeps us sidelined, a lack of a facility, team, or equipment, or living in a climate that limits year-round outdoors activities, we sometimes use excuses to rationalize why our movement practice falters. I found myself doing the same thing when I was benched from hoop dancing when I hurt my back. I whined, complained, and harrumphed that

I couldn't have my dance sessions the way I wanted them. It was very tempting to stop all activity until I could do what I really wanted to do. I know cycling enthusiasts who wouldn't get on a bicycle or a stationary bike because they couldn't ride their favorite lakeside route. How self-defeating is that?

Sadly, I needed to cut back on my hoop dancing, but I chose to find new ways to move my body joyfully just so I could keep receiving the hit of endorphins that come with it. I added arm movements to my yoga practice. I swayed while making dinner. And, my personal favorite: I car-danced. (This is not just for women; I've seen more than one man bust a move in their cars.) Car-dancing is a perfect blend of movement and moxie. It turns an often-odious activity like being stopped at a light into a joyful adventure. It also pushes us to let go of what other people think of us, which is one of our biggest inhibitors to growth. And it reinforces the notion that movement doesn't need to happen only under the best of circumstances.

Find a form of movement that lights your world on fire and do whatever it takes to foster that love on a regular basis. If you loved playing racquet sports as a kid, find a pickleball league in your hometown. If you played soccer or football, join a local team. If you loved playing in the water, go for a swim or even get on a rowing machine and imagine gliding across a river. Be unabashed in your body bliss. Don't tell yourself you are too old, too fat, too whatever to start playing again. I will dance until the day I die, and I hope you do too.

MAKE A DATE

Establishing a mindful movement practice requires planning. You can't assume that 30 to 60 free minutes will just open up in your calendar so you can take good care of yourself. Your day will get full to the brim with other priorities, and your plan to start exercising tomorrow will turn into next week, next month, next year, and then never. Most of us live by our calendars, so one of the most important actions we need to take is to put movement in our schedules just as if it was an appointment. Because it is. It's a date, actually. A date with ourselves. Honor it just as you would an exciting rendezvous with a new or long-term love. Treat your *me time* with reverence. Don't rush through it or skip it because you are tired. In fact, that's precisely when you need movement the most!

Put your movement dates in the calendar and then *show up.*

If you are already a regular mover, congratulations! Maybe your job is not to get started but to take it to the next level. Can you challenge yourself by doing a different activity or sport you may have been hesitant to attempt? Can you improve your performance by challenging yourself even more? Or maybe you can motivate others around you to move more. Start a walking group at work or a volleyball league in the neighborhood! Share your helpful hints with others to get them started and be a source of support or accountability if they need it. Many incredibly lucrative relationships have been established on the golf course or during walk-and-talks; don't discount the power of group movement, not only to positively impact your health but also to catapult your career.

SUPERSTRATEGY: GROUNDING YOUR ENERGY

When I first started learning about mindfulness and mind/body medicine, one of the most important strategies I learned was the practice of grounding. I continue to use it every day to keep me centered. It's a simple but incredibly profound tool anyone can use to disperse energy throughout the body and get it back into balance.

The metaphor of the tree is such a great one when describing the concept of grounding. Did you ever climb trees as a kid? Or play on a tire swing? What kind of tree did you play on? Think about that tree, the one that evokes a positive image in your head. (My favorite is the weeping willow.) Consider all the components of the tree that you can see with your naked eye and those that are hidden from view. You see the leaves, the branches, and the trunk of the tree. But what makes the tree stand tall and endure the occasional wrath of Mother Nature? Its roots, of course. It is the tree's thick root structure that goes deep and wide, well underneath the surface of the ground, that allows it to stand upright and grow larger over the years. Well-rooted trees can withstand the stresses that major storms bring; the wind may cause them to lose their leaves and some of their branches, but their core stays intact. With a solid root structure, they can weather any storm.

So too can you weather the challenges in your own life.

The key to navigating any storm is grounding your energy.

It involves utilizing creative visualization and purposeful breath to emulate that tree and its root structure. Imagine you are that child-hood tree—your fingers are the leaves, your arms are the branches, and your body is the trunk. But you also have energetic roots you do not see that are connected to the earth. Those roots can get weak or disconnected when stress threatens to overtake us.

Grounding is about using your breath to move energy throughout your entire body. Let's practice it now: Imagine your breath directing your energy to wherever you want it to go. Breathe into the lower parts of your lungs. Breathe into your back. Breathe into your belly. Breathe into your arms and fingers. Breathe into your legs and feet. Now, here's the really important part: Breathe into your energetic roots, imagining that you can actually feel your energy going into the earth, deep and wide. Imagine that there is a root coming out of your left foot, your right foot, and the base of your pelvis, like a three-legged stool. As you do this, feel the gravitational pull of the earth, bringing you closer to it. Keep breathing into your roots as they go deeper and wider, imagining what interesting aspects of the earth they are encountering along the way. When you are ready, finish the exercise by breathing from the top of your head once again all the way through your body and into your roots. Complete the process by affirming to yourself that you have everything you need in this moment and you are more powerful than ever before.

By regularly grounding your energy this way, you will possess a stronger center from which to handle any challenges that come your way. I personally utilized this strategy many times as I moved through the painful transitions of job loss, my mother's death, a serious health crisis, financial devastation, and my divorce after almost twenty years of marriage.

It can help you too, not only with the big obstacles, but also with everyday annoyances that may be keeping you from being fully present. When we move energy throughout our bodies and into our roots on a regular basis, we will find peace. Just like your favorite tree, you may lose some leaves and a few branches with the winds of change, but you will remain solid and secure because your root structure is strong.

Establishing and maintaining a movement practice is a foundational aspect of our growth and success. **When we move our bodies regularly and with intention, we are giving ourselves the keys to a gassed-up, properly-maintained body that can take us as far and as high as we want to go.** Let's not limit our dreams because of a lack of energy. We can have more than we ever thought possible, but we've got to move to make it happen.

SELF-REFLECTION:
MOVEMENT

What are your strengths in this focus area?

_____

_____

_____

_____

What are your opportunities for growth?

_____

_____

_____

_____

What specific life experiences came up for you as you read through this chapter? What was the impact to you personally and professionally?

_____

_____

_____

_____

How would improving your activity and awareness in this focus area help you reach your goals?

_____

_____

_____

_____

What are the strategies that resonated with you the most?

- **Move Right Away**
- **Morning Momentum**
- **Movement Toolkit**
- **Rise at the Zeroes**
- **Smart Inefficiency**
- **Squeeze and Release**
- **Joyful Movement**
- **Make a Date**
- **Grounding Your Energy (SuperStrategy)**

What is one action you will take to increase your performance in this area, and by when will you do it?

_____

_____

_____

_____

CHAPTER 4

MEDITATIONS

....

It was just a few short years ago that meditation was largely seen as a cosmic-muffiny, woo-woo activity that only granola-eating, Birkenstock-wearing, tree-hugging hippies did. It was mocked, belittled, and ignored. Mainstream culture is now on board with this once-relegated-to-the-fringes practice thanks to voluminous scientific research that validated meditation's effectiveness, as well as several high-profile case studies of successful mindfulness practitioners (e.g. Jerry Seinfeld, Lady Gaga, Clint Eastwood,

Nicole Kidman, LeBron James, Rupert Murdoch, and of course Oprah, just to name a few). Business leaders now meditate. Elite athletes meditate. Soldiers meditate. Students meditate. Several of your co-workers meditate. Your next-door neighbor probably meditates. The numbers continue to grow.

According to David Gelles' brilliant book "Mindful Work,"[7] on June 6, 1981, Steve Jobs was in Boston about to make an important presentation to thousands of early technology adopters at an event called Applefest. Jobs needed to knock it out of the park to secure Apple's position as a global leader in the tech marketplace. A lot was on the line. Just minutes before he was going to take the stage, Steve snuck away to meditate on the concrete floor backstage, much to the chagrin of the panicked event host who couldn't find him. A few moments later, Jobs opened his eyes, casually walked onstage, and performed like a rock star. Steve Jobs was arguably one of the most successful, innovative, emulated business leaders in modern times, and he thought it was perfectly appropriate to plop down on the floor and sit in silence for a few minutes before delivering a big performance. This example alone is quite an endorsement for the power of meditation. But Steve was not the only leader who tapped into the power of mindfulness to create amazing results.

I grew up in Chicago, and my heart belonged to the Cubbies, the Bears, and my beloved Bulls. My friends and I watched nearly every single Bulls game during those awe-inspiring years of the Michael Jordan dynasty. Sportscasters such as Johnny Red Kerr of WGN-TV would take any opportunity to playfully tease head coach Phil Jackson about his unconventional leadership practices. It was common knowledge that Jackson was a practicing Zen Buddhist who worked with mindfulness expert George

Mumford to incorporate meditation techniques into team practices. Jackson would have the team perform breathing exercises together, tune into the one "team mind", and even had occasional practices where the players would move in silence or in total darkness. Phil was often needled by the media for his unusual antics, but they didn't laugh anymore when he was responsible for six championship seasons. And they *really* didn't laugh at him when he did it again a few years later—five more times!—with the Los Angeles Lakers. Phil ended up becoming the winningest coach in the NBA; I highly recommend his book, "Eleven Rings," to learn more about his mindful leadership approach.[8]

Meditation clearly has found a home in the hallways of industry and on the playing fields of professional sports. It is also finding enormous success in helping veterans address chronic debilitating pain from trauma and PTSD. Teachers across the nation are instructing students in mindfulness instead of serving up punishment to address negative behavioral issues.

When we can intentionally manage our thoughts, we are better able to manage our actions.

Meditation is no longer the quiet secret kept on the mountaintops, at the ashrams, or in the funky New Age workshops. It has slowly, steadily, and permanently become a go-to strategy to promote high performance on the playing field, in the boardroom, on stages, and in schools.

Why?

Because it works.

I could spend the next fifty pages highlighting the many mind-blowing research studies that prove the power of mindfulness and meditation on sleep, concentration, pain management, blood pressure control, empathy, decision-making, and a whole host of other parameters. However, it's more important to use this opportunity to give you real-world strategies you can immediately use to fundamentally improve your performance at work and at home.

If meditation is so amazing at developing our brains, calming our stress responses, and helping us live more powerfully, why isn't everyone doing it? Here are some common responses I hear when asking people if they have ever considered meditating.

"I know it's important, and I wish I could, but …

- **"I don't have time."** This is a flimsy excuse because no one is forcing you to meditate for an hour a day. Or even a half hour. Or even ten minutes. We all have the same amount of time to allocate to whatever pursuits we value. In his documentary, "I Am Not Your Guru"[9], Tony Robbins said, "If you don't have ten minutes, you don't have a life." I couldn't agree more. If you can't wake up ten minutes earlier, then you should stop reading this book right now and gift it to someone who has big dreams and a desire to get there.

- **"I don't know how."** This isn't brain surgery. I'm not asking you to perform some wackadoo, alternate-nostril yogic breathing process. I'm asking you to sit and breathe. You sit and breathe every single day, thousands of times a day. I'm simply inviting you to be conscious of that activity. If you want support on what to do with your mind while you are sitting and breathing, you can always attend a class, read a book, listen to a guided meditation, or download an app. Ignorance is no excuse for not starting this practice. There are just way too many options to help you over the initial learning (or to be more precise, comfort) curve.

- **"I can't sit still"** or **"my mind moves too fast."** These are my favorite excuses. I have the same response every single time I hear it. Then that is *exactly* why you need to start a practice! It's like saying you'll lose those pesky 25 pounds *before* you start going to the gym. No, you go to the gym first and *then* you lose the weight, not the other way around. You, like every other person in the history of the world who started a meditation practice, will initially find it challenging to sit still for an extended period. Your mind will race. It will hurl random thoughts you haven't thought of in years. It will remind you of the pressing tasks you need to do. ("Don't forget to pick up the dry cleaning on the way home!") It will replay a conversation you had hours beforehand. It will relive last night's cliffhanger from your favorite television show. Your mind (or more precisely, your ego) will *hate* that it is quieting itself. It doesn't like that; it fears that. It kicks in with a vengeance to keep you from settling into silence. Expect it. Just because it's going to be uncomfortable for a while doesn't mean you shouldn't do it.

Any other excuses? Send me an email and I promise I'll give you a solution to your so-called obstacle.

Let's take a moment of honest self-assessment: How focused are you? Do you table the less-than-important tasks and bring your full attention on one critical activity, or are you constantly being pulled from one beeping-glowing-ringing device after another, barely able to keep track of where your mind is and what it was supposed to be working on? In my work as a consultant, I have found that overcoming distractions to improve focus is the *biggest* priority for employees in all industries and roles. When we learn how to focus on what is important and remove distractions, we harness our energies toward only those tasks that have the greatest impact to us professionally and personally. Other less important tasks fall by the wayside.

AT HOME

....

Establishing a meditation practice at home is like taking a mini-vacation every single day. Give yourself the gift of calm and presence.

START WITH THE BREATH

The easiest way to start and maintain a powerful meditation practice is through the breath. Focus on the breath and how it feels going in and out of your body. The breath is LIFE, so draw your attention to it. The one you are taking *right now.* How does it feel to inhale deeply? What does it feel like in your chest? In your belly? In your shoulders? In your nostrils? How does it feel when you exhale fully? Can you feel yourself relaxing a little bit more? Do you let go of just a little more stress? Does it clear your mind of the chatter, if only for a moment? What happens in between the breaths? Do you allow for equal spaces in between the inflow and outflow?

When we bring our attention to our breath on a regular basis, we are training our brains to think of one thing at a time. Sure, random thoughts will come in and out of our consciousness; however, over time we start strengthening our focus so we can combat the endless onslaught of distraction that surrounds us.

When all else fails, *breathe.*

Our bodies are wildly different from each other, not only in how they look but how healthy they are and how well they perform. Yet, the breath is the great equalizer. It's the foundational element from which all other activity stems. Without the breath, we no longer exist on the physical plane. It is worthy of reverence and examination. **It is your primary go-to strategy in improving your mindful performance.**

MEDITATION-IN-A-MINUTE

In Chapter 3, I shared the idea of establishing a Morning Momentum routine whereby you take your first several minutes of each day and mindfully implement strategies from the Movement, Meditations, and Manifestations areas. But your meditation practice doesn't need to stop in those first few waking moments. Whenever you find yourself with an extra minute, use it to sit or stand quietly and become conscious of your breath. Resist the urge to pick up your smartphone and see what nonsense is scrolling through your Facebook feed. (See Chapter 9 to learn more about how to create mindful moments with your machines.) When you are waiting for the light to turn green, breathe. When you are waiting in the doctor's office, breathe. When you are standing in line in the grocery store, breathe. When you are waiting for your staff meeting to begin, breathe. You don't need to squeeze in one more email. It can wait. Your Meditation-in-a-Minute is more important.

Peace comes one minute at a time, one breath at a time.

Be selfish with your downtime. See any still moments as opportunities to strengthen your focus and reduce your stress. Paradoxically, you will become *more* productive and a better performer when you take on fewer lower-value activities.

MINDPOWER CALISTHENICS

If you are the kind of person who thinks a meditation practice is for sissies (even though I've previously referenced corporate visionaries and sports superstars who proudly perform it), then I invite you to reframe the entire practice as something a little more palatable: MindPower Calisthenics. That is what mindful performance really is. It's about consistently performing the fundamental exercises that strengthen the power of your mind.

Meditation is like doing push-ups for your brain.

The stronger your mind becomes in its ability to quiet the distractions, improve clarity, and perform more complex decision-making, the more money you'll have in the bank.

Whenever you feel like you don't have time to perform your mental exercise regimen, consider the many benefits you will receive. Imagine yourself sitting around a table with your colleagues or your competition and being the person at the top of the leaderboard. Or the one who has an enviable, stress-free life. Or one of the people who has the freedom to choose how to spend the day. When you perform MindPower Calisthenics every day, you'll be that person. Start working out the six inches between your ears today!

AT WORK

....

Creating meditative moments at work will dramatically improve your ability to tap into deeper levels of creativity and problem-solving as well as foster lucrative relationships with your team, top leadership, customers, and key influencers.

MENTAL DEFRAG

If you are like me, you may be old enough to remember the days when we had to perform regular maintenance and space utilization on our clunky desktops and laptops by performing a process called defragmentation. Defragging our computers was an extremely time-consuming process that could take several hours before we were operational again. We'd watch the colored squares that represented our computer's brain move around, get reorganized, and optimized. The objective of the defrag was to remove the excess spaces that ate up our CPU power, condense the bits and bytes together, and free up big chunks of open space to process larger amounts of data. Technological advances no longer require us to manually execute the digital reorganization, but the analogy still holds true for our time in the office.

When you find yourself feeling sluggish at work—just like our computers used to become—take a break and defrag your brain. With every inhale, imagine those extraneous, unnecessary chunks of distraction are getting reallocated to a special mental folder called "The D File" (D for distraction). With every exhale, imagine that your thinking capacity is growing as those distracted thoughts are filed away. Inhale: Move the chunks of thoughts to the mental folder. Exhale: Expand your processing power. Do this activity for a few minutes before starting any new project that requires deeper thinking, and you will find that your communication, innovation, and problem-solving abilities will soar. You'll simply have more focused processing power with which to create!

OUTCOME ENERGIZATION

Our minds are incredible computing devices. Everything we generate in our inner and outer worlds—good and bad—started with a thought. Sometimes our minds give us what we need; other times, they can play silly games. They can convince us of the presence of threats that aren't there. They can flood us with cringe-worthy "what if" scenarios that paralyze us from acting. And they can deny us confidence and self-esteem because of limited thinking we developed early on in our childhoods. I still remember my odious fourth-grade art teacher, Mrs. Carver, telling me that I "had no artistic talent". If Mrs. Carver is still alive, I have but three words for her: "Proved you wrong!" That silly, misinformed, small-minded comment stayed with me *for years* and colored future opportunities for me because I constantly told myself that "I wasn't creative". It turns out I just wasn't as adept at clay figurines, pencil drawings, and watercolor abstracts. Despite Mrs. Carver's hurtful, incorrect comments, I excel at literary creativity, comedy, and stage performance. (I'll be honest; more than once I have fantasized about tapping her on the nose with a few of my literary awards.)

What programs got installed in your psyche that you wish weren't there? Do you have any messages rolling around in your brain that may be sabotaging you?

- "It won't work out the way I want it to; nothing ever does."

- "I bet I get passed up for the promotion."

- "I don't have what it takes."

- "I never win."

- "I don't have the energy."

How can you start changing the negative programming you received? Rewiring your brain takes work, and you may want to consider chasing after some of the nastier issues with the help of a mental health professional who can help you unpack it all.

However, here is one activity you can do immediately to start executing updated, empowered mental programs. Perform a multi-sensory meditation prior to the next time you have an important event, meeting, audition, or interview. You will mentally pre-pave the outcome you desire prior to it becoming a reality.

Energize your intentional future with your whole body and mind.

Close your eyes for a few minutes and truly *feel* the following aspects of your experience, before they happen in the three-dimensional world:

- **SEE** the people you are going to interact with and their positive reactions to you. See them giving you the offer you want or the outcome you desire. See yourself being calm, confident, and highly competent. See every detail of the successful event, from the smallest detail on up.

- **HEAR** yourself saying the perfect words at the perfect time. Hear others asking meaningful questions—and your intelligent responses to those questions. Hear the applause.

- **TASTE** the healthy meal you are going to have before your event. Savor the nutritious, delicious flavors on your tongue. Taste the coffee or glass of water you'll drink. Taste the mint in your mouth before you step into the limelight.

- **SMELL** the fresh scent of your clean clothes. Smell the hallway and space you'll confidently walk into. Smell the delicious celebratory dinner you will enjoy after your huge win.

- **TOUCH** the handshakes of your counterparts. Touch your reporting masterpiece or the microphone in your hand. Touch the big, fat check made out to you.

You can influence your outcomes by confidently declaring your intention and feeling the results with all your senses.

PRE-PERFORMANCE PREP

Mental preparation is some of the most important work we can do before stepping up to perform in any way—from presenting for a few key influencers in a conference room to being onstage in front of thousands. My experience is that the time immediately preceding a performance is the most excruciating. That is when butterflies show up in our bellies, our throats close, our hearts pound, our heads spin, our legs lock up, and our necks and shoulders get tight. Our mental abilities can suffer because of all these intense physical manifestations of stress.

How can you use mindfulness and meditation to combat the pre-event jitters? First, make sure you take good care of yourself the night before. Eat a healthy dinner; don't try any exotic cuisine for the first time on the night before the big event. Ease up on alcohol consumption so you get a better night's sleep. Take a relaxing hot shower or bath to get you ready for bedtime. Turn off all your devices and perform the Outcome Energization strategy described earlier, your mental movie that runs through every single positive detail of the next day.

- Imagine yourself waking up feeling refreshed, fantastic, and enthusiastic. Imagine yourself wearing your favorite outfit and looking phenomenal.

- Imagine arriving at your location on time, safe and sound. Imagine everyone being incredibly responsive to you.

- Imagine the outcome you desire in gorgeous technicolor.

All of this is done *before* you go to sleep.

On the big day, put some good fuel in your body (more on that in Chapter 11). On your drive to the office, forego the typical music or talk radio and just be with your thoughts. Don't obsess over practicing every detail; frankly, if you don't know your content by then, you aren't going to know it. Instead, use the silence to reinforce your vision for a successful outcome. Obviously, give yourself plenty of time to arrive safely and calmly.

When you are about to enter the arena (whatever that may be— from a conference room to a ballroom), use your mind to visualize yourself as that childhood tree from the section on grounding in Chapter 3. Can you see the tree in your mind's eye? Can you notice the leaves, the branches, and the trunk? Now, can you imagine its complex, deep root structure that you can't see underground? Those roots that go deep and wide are its foundation. The roots are what gives it structure, stability, and life itself. They spread out and dive deeply into the ground. Just as you are about ready to start your performance, imagine that you are that tree. Breathe deeply into the lower part of your chest. Send your breath further down into your belly, lower back, and hips. Breathe into your roots in your legs and pelvis. Imagine that breath going all the way through your body, past the floor and foundation of the space you are in, and deep into the earth. By slowly breathing into your roots, you will find that your nervous energy will dissipate and allow you to think clearly when showtime comes.

Finally, take a big, hungry breath and settle into a state of receptivity and trust, knowing you have everything you need to knock it out of the park. Trust that your vision will become a reality—or something even better will emerge!

A positive mindset creates positive results.

ALL DAY

····································

Here are some simple but incredibly powerful meditation techniques you can employ anytime, anyplace, that will activate your relaxation response and bring about calm, focus, and energy.

BODY SCAN

The body scan technique is a mindfulness strategy you can use to bring yourself back into the present moment and improve your well-being. I liken it to a sci-fi trick that magically improves one's physical, mental, and emotional states, all in a manner of a few minutes.

The body scan allows you to mentally check in with your body from the top of your head all the way through to the bottoms of your feet, looking for any place that may be sore, tight, or uncomfortable in any way. Start at the head, and scan your brain, eyes, mouth, nose, ears, cheeks, mouth, jaw, and neck. Soften any spots that are tense. Relax those tight edges. Continue down your shoulders, arms, wrists, hands and fingers, releasing any stress that has accumulated there. Scan your chest, back, belly, and hips, giving any attention to muscles or organs that seem needful. Stretch, twist, and breathe into the places calling out for attention. Continue downward through your pelvic floor, your legs, knees, ankles, and feet. Wiggle your toes and do some foot circles to release the tension.

Since everybody is different, your body scan will indicate different remedies at any given moment. Maybe your scan tells you that you need something to eat or drink soon. Maybe it tells you that you would benefit from having an icepack or heating pad on your lower back when you get home. Maybe it is reminding you that you are unwittingly clenching your teeth. Maybe it's nudging you to do a little more physical activity. Your body scan will not only give you clues as to what you can to do improve any physical discomfort, but it will also help you consciously relax yourself so you can be more mentally present. Our bodies can distract us from quality mind-work if we don't properly pay attention to their needs.

Consider doing a body scan every time you go from one environment to another. It's a terrific way to close out a phase of your day and open yourself up to be fully present in the upcoming space. For example, perform a body scan when you arrive at work, when you sit down for a meeting, when you are waiting to pick up your kids from school, when you are done with dinner, and anytime you are transitioning from one space to another. You will find that · regular body scanning will make you a better listener, a sharper responder, a more patient participant, and a more creative innovator. It will also tell you which situations make you tense and which make you feel relaxed. This awareness helps you anticipate and modify your reactions.

Our minds can play tricks on us all day long, but our bodies never lie. High achievers keep their vehicles running strong and going long, and performing body scanning as a regular part of their day, every day, will help them get there.

EMOTIONAL AUDIT

Awareness is an essential key to mindfulness. It is Step One from which all other opportunities for conscious choice spring. One strategy to strengthen your awareness muscle is regularly performing an emotional audit, or what I call the "In This Moment" exercise. It can pop you out of a funk very quickly instead of wasting several hours when something (or someone) unpleasant occurs. Once you are aware of where you are emotionally, you can decide to change it, improve it, or, if you like, ignore it altogether.

Suppose your body scan showed you that you are tense after a committee meeting. The next time you have a negative reaction resulting from something that happened to you or around you, complete the following process:

1. "In this moment, I am feeling X". Suspend judgment of yourself and others and simply observe your current emotional state as if you are a scientist conducting a self-experiment. Don't let yourself get away with a generalization that you are feeling mad, sad, or bad. Be specific. Are you restless? Agitated? Annoyed? Resentful? Fearful? Overwhelmed? Disappointed? Hopeless? Name it.

2. Once you have identified what you *really* feel, ask yourself the following question: "Does feeling X serve me and my life vision (or goal, mission, highest good)?"

3. If the answer is no—which it likely will be—ask a follow-up question: "Am I ready to *let go* of this feeling?" Sometimes the answer is no! We can get caught in a seemingly-infinite loop of negativity where, for some reason, we get nourished by our dysfunction. Maybe on one level it is more convenient for us to stay in a place of blame rather than empowerment. (It's a lot easier to stay in a victim mentality state, which is why so many people opt for it.) We are *mal*nourished by this mindset. Deeper dives into mindfulness are often seen as simple, but they certainly aren't always easy.

4. Once you have committed to consciously improving your emotional state, ask yourself, "What *one* action can I take that will up-level my emotion?" Maybe the answer is to take a walk outside for a few minutes. Or maybe you need to have a tough conversation with someone. Maybe you just need to eat a snack! (Getting the "hangries" is real.) Whatever the answer may be, don't try to catapult yourself from a Grade A funk to unbridled ecstasy. It's impossible. Give yourself permission to feel fragile and take steps to shore up your feelings of vulnerability. Simply acknowledge how you feel, confirm that the current emotional state is not ultimately serving you, commit to making it better, and ...

take one single action in support of a better attitude.

Minute by minute and choice by choice, when you execute the "In this moment" emotional audit, you'll find yourself far more present and pleasant with yourself and others.

SUPERSTRATEGY:
FOCUS ON THE BMI

Whenever I find myself stranded at an airport, I'll often strike up a conversation with my fellow travelers. Once the subject comes around to what we do for a living, people often ask for my top recommendations to promote high performance. Focusing on the BMI is definitely one of the top three strategies I recommend. It is so simple and yet so powerful that every single person on the planet should start using it. NOW. *That's* how good it is.

Let's first dispense with the assumption. When I reference Focusing on the BMI, I am not referring to the Body Mass Index measurement that supposedly tells you how fat you are. The mission-critical BMI to which I am referring stands for three aspects that are truly transformational: Breath, Message, and Image. Let's look at each of the three and how you can use them to instantly improve your health, get centered, and give you a jump-start on manifesting your fabulous future reality.

Breath

If your body is a vehicle, then your breath is the mechanism that transports energy throughout that vehicle. It's an ever-present source of fuel that quiets our restless minds and triggers the relaxation response. When something stressful is taking place, we tend to fall back into shallow breaths, robbing our brains and bodies of precious oxygen. *Breathe.* When you find yourself struggling with your current situation, *breathe.* Whether it's an annoying frustration in the grocery store or enduring the unimaginable agony of loss, take a few moments just to stop, ground, and breathe. Count to three with each inhale, hold for a moment, and exhale for a count of three. Even just a few rounds of conscious breathing will reset your mind and engage that all-important parasympathetic nervous system to manage the "rest and digest" function. Once you tap into the breath, you are now ready to follow it up by flooding your psyche with positive messages that are worthy of you and your greatness. (More on the power of messages in Chapter 8.)

Message

What messaging do you want in your head when you are in a high-stress or high-stakes situation? Do you want to be passive and let your unconscious mind install the mental program? Can you imagine that your unconscious mind will be in your best interests, telling you things like, "Relax", "Trust", "You're amazing", or "You've got this"? It's not going to do that. Instead, the niggling voice of fear or doubt will chime in. When we are sloppy with our thoughts, our unconscious minds tell us, "It's not going to work", "Everything sucks", "I never get what I want", or "I'm going to fail".

Instead of relying on chance in the hopes you'll stumble upon something positive or affirming, intentionally declare it.

I study improvisational comedy and love how much it aligns with my teachings in mindful performance. One of the core principles in improv is to start each scene with a strong declarative statement: "I feel ...", "I think ...", "I am ...", "I love ...", "I hate ...". By doing so, we help our scene partners quickly understand who we are and what our objective is. One of the weakest ways to start a scene is by asking a bunch of questions or being noncommittal about our characters. Making positive declarations helps to firmly plant the scene so we can advance and expand in ways that weave a rich (and often hilarious!) tapestry for the audience.

The same holds true for each of us in our own lives. We get to decide how our scenes are going to look. Are we going to start them with a negative declaration ("I'm having a bad day!") and then wonder why our day continues to be so unpleasant? We start our life-scenes in the way that supports a magnificent, rich, highly-entertaining episode if we choose to make positive declarations. These include "I'm confident!", "I trust that all is going to work out exactly as it should!", "I've got all that I need to be successful", and the best one of all, "I'm *grateful*".

Image

After you have executed the Breath and the Message portions of the Focus on the BMI SuperStrategy, it's time to finish it out with the I–the Image. What is the image of success you are choosing to see in your mind's eye? Are you playing the mental movie that shows you succeeding at every turn, or is the image you have in your head one of overwhelm, stress, fatigue, fear, and failure? Are you using your imagination to activate the sensations of success? Can you recall an image of a perfect setting that allows you to fully relax? Where is your happy place? Be relentless in your mission to flood your mind with positive imagery.

Focusing on the BMI is your own personal "Get Out of Funk Jail Free Card". It will put you back in the driver's seat of your destiny. It will instantly bring you to a state of presence and peace. It will set you free from the binds of anxiety and stress. And all it takes is a few minutes to breathe deeply, create self-affirming messaging, and visualize calming, empowering images.

One of the greatest thinkers of our time was Albert Einstein. He once said, "No problem can be solved from the same level of consciousness that created it." All the powerful meditation practices included in this chapter enable you to solve the problems you have in your life from a different level of consciousness—one that is quiet, calm, and totally in command of your mind, body, and spirit.

SELF-REFLECTION:
MEDITATIONS

What are your strengths in this focus area?

_____

_____

_____

_____

What are your opportunities for growth?

_____

_____

_____

_____

What specific life experiences came up for you as you read
through this chapter? What was the impact to you personally
and professionally?

_____

_____

_____

_____

How would improving your activity and awareness in this focus area help you reach your goals?

_____

_____

_____

_____

What are the strategies that resonated with you the most?

- **Start with the Breath**
- **Meditation-in-a-Minute**
- **MindPower Calisthenics**
- **Mental Defrag**
- **Outcome Energization**
- **Pre-performance Prep**
- **Body Scan**
- **Emotional Audit**
- **Focus on the BMI (SuperStrategy)**

What is one action you will take to increase your performance in this area, and by when will you do it?

_____

_____

_____

_____

.

CHAPTER 5

MANIFESTATIONS

....

My mother's favorite book was "Think and Grow Rich" by Napoleon Hill. (This classic was originally published in 1937.) It sat on her nightstand for thirty years, that same old $1.95 weathered copy. It contains great wisdom on how to create success financially and otherwise. My favorite quote is "Whatever the mind of man can conceive and believe, he shall achieve." Our minds are powerful creators, and if we really want to create success previously unseen, we need to utilize our minds in a conscious manner.

Manifestation is defined as "an event, action, or object that clearly shows or embodies something". As you create the life and business you desire and deserve, purposeful manifestation will guide you to take consistent, specific mental actions that embody your success—as if you already have it. You will use your mindpower to move into vibrational alignment with your vision before it takes place. I like to think of it as a mental blueprint. Just as architects create structures on paper before they become reality ...

you will create the life and career of your dreams in your mind first.

If the specifications of a new construction project aren't written down, contractors responsible for the actual creation of the building don't know what to build. In your life, the conscious act of manifestation will help you know what to do to create your success as clearly and efficiently as possible.

AT HOME

Some of your most important mental acts of creation will be performed in the comfort of your own home.

SUPERSTRATEGY:
STATEMENT OF INTENTION

As a keynote speaker, I am in front of tens of thousands of people every year, many of whom are quietly dissatisfied with their lives. They are tolerating every day instead of reveling in it. They wish they were healthier, richer, happier, calmer, and more balanced. Yes, they have moments of satisfaction, levity, and success, but overall, they aren't living up to what they thought their lives would be like.

Yet, when I ask them what they want, they often shrug their shoulders and say, "I don't know." Well, if you don't know what you want, how can you expect to get it? Imagine going to a restaurant and the server asks you for your order, to which you reply, "I don't know. Bring me whatever." And then she puts a plate of slimy liver and onions in front of you. Sure, it will fill the emptiness in your belly, but it certainly isn't what you wanted. You say, "I don't want this!" and she asks you for what you would like instead, to which you reply, "I don't know, but not that!" A few minutes later she brings you a plate of lutefisk (for my fellow Minnesotans, you know what I'm talking about; the rest of you will need to Google it.) Again, you say, "NO! I want something different!" to which she exasperatedly snaps back, "Hey, if you can't tell me what you want, I can't help you."

Life is the same way.

When you keep complaining about what the Universe delivers to you (stress, poor health, challenging relationships, money woes, sleepless nights and so on) but you can't clearly articulate what you *do* want, then it's your fault for not placing your order.

A *Statement of Intention* is the tool I recommend to gain clarity on what you desire so you may place the order you actually want.

STATEMENT OF INTENTION

Write in the present tense a thoughtful, concise vision of your ideal life. Describe what you want physically, mentally, emotionally, spiritually, financially, vocationally, relationally, and recreationally. Print several copies and place around your living and work spaces. Recite it multiple times a day until it is committed to memory. Continue to energize your Statement of Intention daily, and modify it when your vision changes.

I am so grateful that I now...

_____

_____

_____

_____

Thank you, (God/Higher Power/Universe/Higher Self), for this or something better!

To complete the exercise, take ample time to truly think about what you want in all areas of your life—physically, mentally, emotionally, spiritually, financially, vocationally, relationally, and recreationally. What does the Ideal You look like? Describe yourself in detail. Don't rush through this process—really consider what it is that would genuinely light you up and bring you a sense of profound peace and deep satisfaction. Creating your *Statement of Intention* can be laborious and tedious, but it is well worth the investment of time. If you can't write it down, you can't communicate it. **If you can't communicate it, you can't attract the resources to help you get there.**

Let's walk through the process of putting the *Statement of Intention* into practice. Imagine you want to receive a big promotion at work.

1. Step into the mental dream space to create the future reality you desire in gorgeous technicolor. Imagine every element of your inevitable success (what you look like, how you feel, what you drive, where you live, who you work for, how much money you make, what you do on vacation, how you carry yourself every day, and so on). Get so solid on your vision that you could play it as a movie with you as the director, producer, writer, editor, and star. You could write the script in detail if needed.

   > ***Example:*** *"I am in optimal health and feel more attractive than I ever have before. I feel fantastic and have unlimited energy to do what I want when I want. I live in a beautiful, well-appointed home in a great location that supports my family's needs. I thoroughly enjoy my job, embrace the challenges, and appreciate my company. When my family and I go on vacation, we thoroughly*

enjoy ourselves and create amazing memories. I have more than enough financial resources to provide for my family and me, not only now but also in the future when I want to retire. Every day is filled with a sense of satisfaction for the life I am intentionally creating."

2. Create your summary *Statement of Intention* with the most important aspects defined. Invest the time to wordsmith your vision so it perfectly captures exactly what you want. Make sure your heart skips when you read it. You want it. You ache for it. You will do anything to get it. That's a Statement of Intention worthy of you.

3. Type and print multiple copies of the finished *Statement of Intention*. Put each copy in a conspicuous place where you will see it and read it every single day. (I have mine on my nightstand, by my meditation space, on the bathroom mirror, on my computer monitor, and in my car.) **Recite your *Statement of Intention* every day, multiple times a day, and feel the energy of already having it.** Recite it over and over until you have committed it to memory. Do the mental legwork to get it solidified in your brain. This full embodiment is key to your success.

4. Energize the heck out of your *Statement of Intention* every morning and night. Take several minutes to recite it out loud and feel what it feels like to already have accomplished it. For example, if you are going for your big promotion, feel what it feels like to already be sitting in the new office, making the increased salary, and performing the additional responsibilities. Be in the important meetings. Make compelling presentations to key influencers. Negotiate and close big deals.

5. Make sure you have a current *Statement of Intention* you can read immediately before turning out the lights and immediately upon waking. This is your blueprint for success. It is your framework upon which everything is built. Read it several times every day to commit it to memory. You will find yourself feeling more in control of the direction of your life and better able to weed out those superfluous, distracting activities that are hogging your time. If there is anything on the *Statement of Intention* that loses power as you read it or is no longer relevant, edit it and reprint. Your recipe for having more is right at your fingertips. Use it.

Create it. Write it. Memorize it. Energize it. Acquire it.

Recall the definition of manifestation I shared at the start of this chapter: "an event, action, or object that clearly shows or embodies something." Every time you energize and embody your *Statement of Intention* with intentional thought and multi-sensory feeling, you are one step closer to making your mental reality your physical reality.

THOUGHT ENERGY

Energy begets energy. If you put X amount of force against a stationary object, it will move the distance equal to X amount. Conversely, if you starve a process of energy, nothing will get created.

Inertia is the destroyer of dreams.

Your thought energy is the most important type of energy you can feed, because it will give you a direction on where to focus your efforts. When we aren't deliberate in the expression of our thought energy, we can find ourselves scattered and moving into reactive mode throughout our day. Time gets stolen from us, and before we know it, we haven't put forth the necessary effort to create what we really want. We are too busy responding to what others want or we are putting out fires.

To get a sense of the health of your current thought energy, take a spin through your social media pages, your email sent folder, and your text messages. You put some thought into putting those words out into the world, and they are good representations of your current mindset. Are your words for the most part positive, hopeful, and encouraging? Or not?

By prioritizing and leveraging your thought energy every single day—throughout the entire day—you are getting into the driver's seat on the journey of your life.

DELIBERATE LIVING

There are only two ways to live: deliberately or by default. You either decide to consciously create the life you desire based on the recipe you decide, or you sit back and wait for someone or something else to create it for you. Yes, deliberate living requires significantly more investment of thought energy and physical energy. It requires you to say "no" to things you really want to do or would soothe you in the short-term. It requires you to toughen up when you emotionally invest in an outcome and it hasn't yet come to fruition.

Deliberate living requires you to draw a line in the sand and say definitively *what is* and *isn't* acceptable to you. It also may require you to remove those forces—or people—who are not in alignment with your direction. All these challenges are significant and require a level of commitment and character that not everyone possesses. However, tackling these challenges is the only way you will get the life you want.

Notice the moments when you are choosing to live deliberately and extend those periods until you have established a new, more empowered thought pattern.

AT WORK

When you intentionally manifest at work and consciously plan each day, you will differentiate yourself from your less-than-mindful colleagues and supercharge your performance.

RESOURCE READINESS

Have you ever bought anything from Ikea and tried to put it together without the right tools or sufficient direction? It's a total nightmare. You end up spending an inordinate amount of time completing the task because it takes what seems like forever to try to figure out the instructions. You can make costly mistakes and end up wanting to throw that thing out the window before you finally get it assembled. All it takes is one missing piece, one confusing instruction, or one wrong tool to make the entire project go off the rails. However, when you have every single piece you need as well as the tools, space, and instructions to put it together, you can do more than you ever thought possible. (In my early 20s I put together an entire entertainment center which had no less than 800,000 pieces.)

The vision you have for your career, business, relationships, and personal health is just like that Ikea project. It requires the effective utilization of several resources to make it a reality. This not only includes a consistent mental investment of time in pre-paving your future, but it also involves ensuring that all resources you need to manifest your vision are in place.

- Have you received sufficient training in core competencies?

- Are you utilizing the latest time-saving tools and technologies?

- Do you have powerful mentors and advocates in place to assist you?

Define all the resources you need to realize your *Statement of Intention* and put a specific plan in place—with due dates—to acquire each one. You'll be on your way in no time!

WHO'S GOING TO DO WHAT BY WHEN

I started my professional career as a temporary employee. If you've ever been a temp, you know the kind of nightmare it can be. You pop around from job to job, not knowing what you are going to find or what will be asked of you.

When I entered the workforce, I quickly discovered that I had an aptitude for getting things done quickly and successfully. It wasn't that hard. I just had to identify what needed to get done, who was going to do it, and by when. Communicating these directives in a way that motivated a team to execute them is an art, especially for a young woman; my nickname back in those days was "The Velvet Hammer". In fact, when I moved up through the ranks of temp to administrative assistant (back then we were called secretaries) to project coordinator to manager and beyond, I realized one of the most important aspects of finding success was to have a project manager's mindset.

The essence of managing and completing any initiative boils down to one simple refrain: *Who's going to do what by when.*

If you think of your career as its own project, then you can get clarity on what actions you need to take to make it succeed. No matter how big the initiative, it can always be broken down into smaller chunks, identifying the three keys: WHO, WHAT, and WHEN.

For example, if you want to complete a work-related course, break the process down into chunks and figure out the Who, What and When. "I (WHO) will contact the Staff Development Department to start the course (WHAT) by the end of this month (WHEN)." This systematized way of thinking will enable you to tackle any undertaking no matter how lofty. If you are in leadership, this strategy will also help you keep your team's activities on the fast track, so they don't fall behind because of unclear expectations, mushy boundaries, or disengagement.

POST-IT POWER

How will you implement this notion of manifestation? How can you take your dreams of improved profitability, productivity, and purpose from thought to reality? As I mentioned earlier, your *Statement of Intention* is critical in solidifying your vision. Your Resource Readiness also needs to be in place, and your mindset needs to be one of a Who/What/When project manager.

If you are like me, you review the next day's schedule before you go to bed to prepare yourself mentally for the activities and meetings you will be having. As you look at your calendar and consider how you want the day to unfold, jot down on a post-it note one, two or three critical tasks you *will* perform the next day. Stick that post-it note on the back of your phone—you *know* you'll always have that nearby—and don't remove it until you complete your tasks. This strategy is a simple but powerful clarifier with built-in self-accountability.

The humble post-it note is your doorway to massive performance and productivity.

By identifying these important focal areas every single day, you will relieve your mind of worry about what you *should* be doing and free it up to actually *do* it.

ALL DAY

As you infuse your day with mindful manifestations, you may just start to feel like a magician or the character Neo from "The Matrix": You will be bending your realities like clay, creating your biggest and best version of yourself. You will be manifesting You 2.0.

SEE THE PARKING SPOT

If you are new to the process of conscious manifestation, I recommend starting with baby steps. Once you find success in small ways, you can up your game to include bigger-ticket items in your work and personal life.

Have you ever been cruising back and forth in a busy parking lot in a vain attempt to snag that elusive, close-to-the-entrance spot? This scenario is a perfect place to start consistently mentally manifesting. The next time you find yourself running an errand, take a few moments before you leave your house to mentally pre-pave the perfect parking spot. Imagine it close to the door waiting there just for you, almost as if it has a "Reserved for Me" sign on it. Don't hope for it to be there; *know* it will be there. Make this a habit when you go out. See the parking spot in your mind's eye before you see the parking spot with your physical eyes. You may not always land "the" spot, but you will see that you will dramatically improve your outcomes over time. Isn't most of the time better than none of the time?

Once you get the hang of mental pre-paving, start tackling bigger objectives. Manifest closing a substantial chunk of business by the end of the week. Manifest receiving the perfect email that will open amazing new doors of possibility. Manifest having a chance encounter with a handsome or beautiful stranger! You never know, and it never hurts to ask, right?

I used this principle a while back in my speaking business. I received an email from a client letting me know that an upcoming speaking event for which I was keynoting was abruptly canceled because of a company restructuring. As a result, I was not going to get paid (at least at that point) for my presentation. I didn't want to lose out on the money, so I immediately put the manifestation principle into action.

I declared that I was going to book *five times* the amount of business that was lost by the end of the week. I voiced my intention aloud to my friend. I described the unexpected business finding its way to me within a matter of days. I imagined the invoice in Quickbooks. I knew it was not a possibility; it was an inevitability. Three days later, a prospective client called me based on a recommendation he'd received years ago. By the end of the conversation, I had a contract on its way to him for exactly five times the amount of lost revenue. When you get into the frequency of manifestation, you can use it for all sorts of interesting creations.

Magic happens when you leverage the power of your mind. Expect it.

What sorts of fun things—parking spots, chance encounters, unexpected income, whatever you want—can you create this month? Seek out those opportunities as you move into mental mastery.

THE COSMIC NOOGIE

When you were a kid, did you ever get (or give) a noogie? If you were so fortunate to have a noogie-free childhood, allow me to explain: A noogie is when someone ferociously rubs their knuckles on the top of another's head to annoy them as much as humanly possible. Second only to The Wedgie, there was nothing more obnoxious to receive from our childhood counterparts. But, you must give it up for the noogie: we paid attention to it. It was a presence that could not be denied. The noogie made itself known.

Similar in power and presence (but not the degree of obnoxiousness) is what I call the Cosmic Noogie. It's when the Universe (or whatever you want to call any force that is beyond your conscious mind) alerts you to act on something important. When you start to practice mindfulness more consistently, you will find that you will receive more and more Cosmic Noogies. At first, they may be nearly-indistinguishable gentle nudges that will pop into your head ("Hey, you should call Greg," or "Go to that networking mixer; you may meet someone important.") Cosmic Noogies can open doors that your conscious mind would otherwise not bring to your attention because they are so minor or "out in left field".

The key to leveraging the power of the Cosmic Noogie is to be present enough to notice it. Did a passing thought or random idea stay in your head for a few seconds longer than usual? Have you heard or read about the same event more than a few times? Do you keep having the same dream? Do you have this needling feeling like you should share your big idea with your boss? These are all Cosmic Noogies.

Once you notice the noogie, commit to acting upon it. Don't blow it off. It's not enough to get the nudge. You need to do what you are being prompted to do. This is where so many people fail. They have a recurring thought or strong intuitive hit and then let their conscious minds (or more accurately, their egos) get in the way of acting on it. Our egos tell us all sorts of lies to avoid losing its hold on us. We tell ourselves we must be imagining things …We shouldn't take risks like that …It's probably a bad idea … It will never work. Blah blah blah. WRONG!

Follow the Cosmic Noogie, dear one. As you refine your mindfulness practices, you will discover that mental awareness and a highly-tuned intuition will spotlight all sorts of juicy opportunities that are in perfect alignment with you and your goals.

SUPERSTRATEGY: GRATITUDE RANT

The practice of gratitude is widely accepted as not only a key to living a satisfied life, but also a powerful tool in creating success, health, and balance. We all know that being grateful is good for us. I liken it to a magic elixir that can transform a bad mood into a good one, scarcity into abundance, and a mediocre existence into an amazing life. Something really does happen with our brain chemicals when we stop focusing on all the horrible things that are going on in our lives (and in the world in general) and look at things more optimistically.

If we know our attitudes are directly correlated with our gratitude, how can we integrate it consistently?

On a scale of one to ten, rate your current levels of satisfaction with your health, wealth, relationships, right livelihood, and home life—with one being a miserable reality that is nearly intolerable and ten being a constant state of contentment and peace. What are your numbers? What would you like them to be? Taking it one step further, how would those who know you personally and professionally describe you? Would you be seen as inspiring, healthy, powerful, successful, well-liked, and blessed? Or would others secretly describe you with less-enviable words such as overwhelmed, frustrated, tired, unhealthy, or stressed? **How are you really showing up for yourself and the world?**

Decide if your current reality is congruent with what you want your life to be. There will always be areas that can be improved upon, but ask yourself if you are often in a state of contentment. If not, your manifestation flow may be blocked by your persistent state of discontent. The good news is that you can remove those jam-blocking mental hairballs anytime you choose by executing the Gratitude Rant strategy.

If you already have a consistent practice of expressing gratitude, whether it's writing in a journal every night, starting each day by declaring three things for which you are grateful, or simply reframing any glass-half-empty moments, then keep doing them! However, you may also want to augment your manifestation process by incorporating the Gratitude Rant into your day.

A rant is a rapid-fire monologue that contains a lot of emotional energy. Whether it's stand-up comedians doing a rant on a subject or the angry person ranting in the terminal gate area about the canceled flight, there is a sense of being "out of one's mind". Words are coming from somewhere other than the logical brain, cascading out seemingly without control. Your gratitude rant can, and should, come from somewhere other than your head as well. Consider stepping away from your devices and other distractions and dive heart-first into gratitude whenever you feel yourself blocked by prosperity energy—doors keep getting slammed in your face, you get passed over for a promotion, opportunities you thought were "in the bag" are no longer even close to the bag.

Ask yourself over and over, **"What am I grateful for?"** or "What is good in my life and in the world?" Just let the words flow out of you, preferably out loud, without filter or conscious thought. Just let them bubble out of you as quickly as possible and continue for as long as you can. Think of the obvious ones (your family, your health, a roof over your head, food in your belly), but also give some time to the more unusual gifts (the smell of rain in the spring, the taste of a fresh scone right out of the oven, the moment your team won the championship, your ability to video chat with your child when you are a thousand miles away). Flood your body and your mind with only those thoughts that make you grateful. Soon your sad-sack attitude will be replaced with a more gracious, receptive tone. Often it is in those times of gentle appreciation for "what is" that the next great idea will hit you or the phone will ring.

What are you grateful for?

Gratitude is magic—magic you know the secret to. **Taking time to consciously appreciate all the gifts we have turns our frowns upside down, which helps us approach new challenges with greater energy and focus.**

The famous quote from the movie "Field of Dreams" was, "If you build it, they will come." It is similar for your creations. Your creation will eventually manifest (or something even better) if you build your dream in your mind first, consistently energize it over time, take purpose-driven actions, stay in a positive mindset with gratitude, and never ever *ever* give up. But only when you harness every single resource toward that singular vision. Leverage the most powerful resource you have to intentionally create more profitability, productivity, and purpose: Your mind.

SELF-REFLECTION:
MANIFESTATIONS

What are your strengths in this focus area?

_____

_____

_____

_____

What are your opportunities for growth?

_____

_____

_____

_____

What specific life experiences came up for you as you read through this chapter? What was the impact to you personally and professionally?

_____

_____

_____

_____

How would improving your activity and awareness in this focus area help you reach your goals?

_____

_____

_____

_____

What are the strategies that resonated with you the most?

- **Statement of Intention (SuperStrategy)**
- **Thought Energy**
- **Deliberate Living**
- **Resource Readiness**
- **Who's Going to Do What by When**
- **Post-it Power**
- **See the Parking Spot**
- **The Cosmic Noogie**
- **Gratitude Rant (SuperStrategy)**

What is one action you will take to increase your performance in this area, and by when will you do it?

_____

_____

_____

_____

CHAPTER 6

MEETINGS

....

Regardless of our career choice, we likely have had the need to at least once sit down across the table or over the telephone with a colleague to have a meeting. Meetings are formal discussions designed to work through one or more (hopefully) important issues. They are a critical component of the collaborative process and necessary for any organization to flourish. Poorly-run meetings are also nearly universally loathed because of their annoying, time-sucking nature. Whether it is a project update meeting in the office or a house rules reminder meeting with your teenage child at the dinner table, knowing how to mindfully conduct a purpose-driven conversation will save you an inordinate amount of time and aggravation. You'll be able to deal with unclear expectations while dramatically improving bottom-line results and relationship dynamics.

AT HOME

Meetings don't just take place in the workplace. Far more important meetings happen within the confines of our own homes with our loved ones. Yet, we aren't really taught how to have those kinds of meetings, instead opting to wing it and hoping we will get the results we want. When that doesn't happen, other behaviors kick in (such as passive aggressiveness or blame). Suddenly we aren't talking about the meeting topic anymore but rather the poor communication habits of the parties involved. Feelings get hurt. Words are said (or not said) that are harmful. Relationships fracture. Stress grows. It's a recipe for disaster, all because we haven't been educated on how to have a mindful meeting at home.

HOUSE MEETING LOGISTICS

When an important discussion is needed at home, treat the logistics of the meeting with the same degree of import you do when hosting meetings at work. Make sure all parties know—even the children—who will be at the meeting, what will be discussed (try to keep it to one or two items, not the laundry list of gripes), where it will be held (preferably in a neutral location), when it will happen, and most importantly, *why* you are calling the meeting.

The more weight you give the importance of the discussion, the more weight others will give it. If you try to have a casual conversation about something that merits more seriousness, then you are setting yourself up to be disappointed at the cavalier reaction you may receive. Springing major issues on people will only cause them to be defensive or disengaged. Rarely will they be as vested as you are, which automatically skews the conversation dynamics. Just imagine—you have been obsessing over having "the talk" for hours, practicing all your best lines in your head, psyching yourself up to go to battle, and your family doesn't have a clue what's about to hit them. That's not playing fair. Instead, let them know you want to carve out a mutually-acceptable time to chat about Topic A and sincerely, respectfully ask them to participate. Be open to what works for them. Don't be tempted to get into the conversation at that point; just redirect any deeper discussions to the allotted time of the meeting. You want them to willingly come to the table · ready to discuss something important to the well-being of your relationship.

Showing respect for the W5 logistics—Who, What, Where, When, and Why—will automatically make for a more meaningful, respectful exchange of thoughts and ideas.

COMPLETE CONVERSATIONS

My experience as a coach has given me a snapshot into hundreds of damaged relationships, many of which are suffering from the effects of having partial conversations. We are creating a half-baked conflict when we don't think through exactly why we are upset or the mitigating circumstances surrounding it, opting instead to blurt out our dissatisfaction in the heat of the moment. We aren't articulating the entire issue because we haven't thoroughly considered it. This is especially true for relationships that are suffering well beyond someone having a bad day or a tough few weeks. We often address only the latest in a series of issues, allowing a dysfunctional relationship to continue without honestly addressing the full scope of the conflict. If you are in this type of relationship either at work or at home, I highly encourage you to get neutral, third-party professional support to unpack the complexity (power dynamics, manipulations, fears and threats, long-term impacts, and so on) to truly understand what kind of *real* conversation needs to happen.

Nearly all the clients I have counseled who go through a breakup admit that they knew they should have ended it long before they did. Instead, they endured years of endless agony, hoping things would change.

Hope is not an effective relationship management strategy.

If they had the clarity and a network of support to assist them earlier on, they could have had one whole difficult conversation instead of two dozen painful half-conversations.

Even for less serious conversations, remember to have the *whole* conversation. That may mean you compliment your children on the activities they do well, in addition to talking about their poor choices. For example, if you want them to be more present at dinnertime instead of being distracted by their devices, remind them about how wonderful it is when they really participate in the family experience by giving an example. Having a whole conversation may mean that you own your role in the conflict more fully. We'll be discussing owning our own messes in Chapter 10.

EMBRACING EMOTION

When you are having a discussion with your loved ones—or anyone else for that matter—don't forget to bring in more than just your words. Saying words without having any authentic emotion fueling them can fall flat in the hearts and minds of those with whom we are trying to communicate. An expression of genuine emotion can be the difference between someone going through the motions versus truly understanding us.

Make sure your emotions come from an honest, non-manipulative place. If we are hurt, we should say, "I am hurt." Don't turn the hurt into anger and then go on the attack by saying, "You always do this. You make me so angry!" That person doesn't *make* you do anything; you have allowed yourself to feel hurt. I encourage people to go deeper than the surface emotion and see what vulnerability lies underneath it. Sure, you can be frustrated, but what's underneath the frustration—worry that you aren't a good parent, fear that you won't be able to handle the challenges facing you, or doubt that you know the "right" approach to take?

Don't be afraid to show your joy as well! So often we damp down our happiness in favor of being perceived as "serious". People are attracted to those who have a sunny disposition. Let your excitement, enthusiasm, and passion come through! People respond most to what they feel, not just to what they hear or see.

Be courageous when embracing your emotion. Use breathing techniques and meditation practices discussed earlier so you can healthfully express any negative feelings without losing control. It takes strong people to own their tender side. Let your empowered emotions be a part of your meetings when appropriate, and you will find that others will share their truths as well. When that happens, you will soon be on the path to true communication and collaboration.

AT WORK

Have you ever had to endure a seemingly endless discussion, only to discover that you sat through an entire hour-long meeting just to talk about having another meeting? Isn't that frustrating? While you may not be able to immediately streamline every single meeting you attend, you can begin to make a difference in the level of performance, output, and time utilization by running your own meetings like a Jedi.

Gallup's report, *State of the American Manager: Analytics and Advice for Leaders*[10], showed that when managers engage in regular meetings with their employees, the employees are almost three times more likely to be engaged compared to those who don't. If you are an organizational leader, please do everyone a favor and train your people on how to conduct effective meetings. Make sure you are doing them yourself as well. You will not only be the most popular person in the office, you'll quickly see a dramatic increase in performance and team unity. This stuff works.

MONEY VALUE OF TIME

When conducting mindful meetings, we need to consider the Money Value of Time. There is a cost an organization pays when a group of people gather together to have discussions versus "doing actual work". Every minute counts. When we make each meeting minute mean something, we are being responsible stewards of the organizational resources.

If you are the facilitator, show up with plenty of time to prepare the room. If you tend to be late, set the start time in your calendar for an earlier time so you are never, ever late. If you called a 9:00 a.m. meeting, then at 9:00 a.m. *on the dot* start the meeting no matter who is around the table. There is always at least one person who honors the process. Don't disrespect them by having them wait for late arrivals. Yes, those first few times you may get grimaces from the latecomers, but that's okay. When they walk in, don't make it a big deal. If they say, "Whoa, you started already!", respond jovially, "Yep, we had a start time of 9:00 and I want to honor everyone's schedule." Just keep going. If they want you to backtrack, politely decline, saying you won't be able to hold to the agenda if you circle back on content you've already discussed. Assure them they will catch up and, if they have any questions after it is over, they can ask you or read the minutes.

When you sense that people are repeating themselves or treading over discussion points that have already been addressed, don't be afraid to say so. With your most polite voice and approachable body language, gently suggest that the issue (not the person) has been appropriately discussed at this point and ask if the discussion (not the person) can move on. Don't make the focus the people talking too much, or you risk insulting them publicly; rather, make time the ultimate master. Blame the clock. Honor the agenda. Tell them you are committed to nudging the group forward to adhere to the meeting timeframes no matter who is talking. That's your job as a responsible facilitator and custodian of the organizational resource of time. The other folks around the table will be eternally grateful to you for your steely resolve, and they will also think twice before running off at the mouth willy-nilly. Projects get completed on time. Relationships flourish. Money is made. People succeed. Everybody wins.

UNIFIED ARRIVAL

How many times have you sat down at a meeting after having rushed to get there? Your mind is still on the conversation you just had or the traffic you just endured, and you are annoyed that you "have to" be at this meeting. You are crabby, hungry, tired, stressed, and not at all prepared to have engaging conversations about the upcoming topic at hand. Guess what? Your negativity is contagious. This sets the tone for the entire meeting: one of disengagement, disappointment, delays, and distraction.

Several highly-successful, forward-thinking companies are now seeing opportunities to combat this productivity-sucking habit by using mindfulness techniques at the start of their meetings. They allow time for people to arrive, not only in body, but also in mind and in spirit.

Take the Eileen Fisher company, for example. When a meeting start time arrives, a facilitator (there should always be someone in charge) rings a bell or chime, signifying that the meeting has begun. For the next minute, everyone around the table stops everything they are doing, and just starts being. They put away their devices, close their eyes, and breathe. Simply breathe. They take those few precious moments to clear their heads of distraction that may still be lurking, allowing them to come to the table with a focused, open mind. After just a minute of silently breathing in unison, everyone feels like they are ready to be present and will contribute far more meaningfully. The facilitator rings the chime once again to signify that the arrival portion is complete, and the discussion can continue as planned. Everybody is finally there to do the work needed.

At your next meeting, consider taking one minute to allow people to quiet their minds, settle into the present moment, and get focused on the objective. Using a timer will help everyone relax and trust that their time isn't being "wasted." Fostering a unified arrival builds cold steel group concentration.

MINDFUL MEETING MASTERY

Hosting a mindful meeting requires much more than reserving a big enough room or sending out a meeting notice. Did you ever look around a meeting room and calculate each person's hourly rate? When you total that up, a meeting could be costing thousands of dollars an hour. If you want to maximize the time, money, and energy it takes to bring a group of people together to discuss an issue, then a certain amount of discipline is required not only on the part of the facilitator but also on each attendee. By investing extra energy in the critical pre- and post-meeting phases, you will not only dramatically improve performance, you'll also be cultivating a much stronger, healthier, more respectful, and more collaborative relationship among the team members.

Do these critical items every time you host a professional gathering:

- **Define the meeting's purpose.** Why are you getting people together in the first place? Is it merely to make your life easier? Meetings should only take place when you are discussing complex issues that cannot otherwise be reasonably handled over email or other methods of collaboration.

- **Identify must-have attendees.** Don't be lazy when it comes to the invitee list. In fact, consider indicating on the invitation *why* each person is being asked to attend and what he or she will be contributing to the discussion. Your colleagues will appreciate you acknowledging their unique value and will be more prepared to have meaningful discussions.

- **Craft the agenda.** Document meeting logistics, who will be in attendance, and the exact start and end times for each section. Allow for some breathing room, but don't be too generic in your scheduling. An agenda that is too general gives people an excuse to skip the meeting.

- **Make scheduling easy.** Consider using a polling website to avoid the email scheduling ping-pong. Identify a few possible meeting dates and times that work with your calendar. Start with the most important attendees and make sure you get them to commit. Then you can send a secondary invitation for tier-two attendees.

- **Assign critical pre-work.** Don't be afraid to ask people for written status reports prior to the meeting. You may get some push-back at the beginning, but by modeling good behavior yourself and showing how much more time is saved, attendees will start doing the front-end legwork. Make this process public and simple to complete so people are more apt to get their reports done.

- **Allow sufficient time.** Don't wait too long to schedule a meeting. Nobody likes last-minute fire drills. It makes you look unprofessional and only undercuts their desire to work collaboratively with you.

- **Be crystal clear.** When the start time arrives, start the meeting, regardless of who is around the table. Thank your attendees and remind them of the purpose of the meeting. Dive into the agenda immediately. (If you want to schedule a few minutes of unified arrival or quick personal sharing, then do so. But treat it like any other item on the agenda; don't let it get out of hand.) This is about business, not play time or screen time. You can (and should) be pleasant, but don't be overly casual.

- **Make the clock your co-host.** Have a clock visible so everyone can see you will be managing each agenda item to its assigned timeframe. A minute or two before the next section is slated to start, politely indicate to the person speaking that time is wrapping up for this section. If more time is needed, either decide to steal a few minutes from another section or table the discussion for another conversation. Do *not* go over the allotted time of the meeting. Ever. It's rude and will come back to haunt you in the form of disengagement.

- **Follow up immediately.** Track all decisions and actions that stem from the meeting, and distribute the minutes within 72 hours. Be specific as to the expectations that were discussed and the timeframes for completion. Invest the time to make those meeting minutes rock. You want people to read them, forward them, and refer to them.

- **Don't allow slackers.** If/when people don't do what they should do, from skipping the meeting altogether to multitasking during the meeting to blowing off their action items, directly communicate with them in private about how their choices are harming the group. Be understanding, be neutral, and be specific about what is required. If there is a legitimate reason as to why they shouldn't be involved, then take that information and act accordingly. But don't let anyone sandbag your efforts. Other attendees will be watching how you handle the slackers. Don't give them a reason to be one too.

Yes, running a mindful meeting takes additional time on the part of the host. It requires forethought, organization, effective communication skills, and discipline. However, when your attendees realize you mean business when it comes to hosting ninja-like meetings, they will make time for you and your event. Over time, your organizational influence quotient will skyrocket, and you will have people clamor to be on such a high-performance team! (OK, maybe they won't be clamoring, but they also won't need to be dragged to the conference room kicking and screaming.)

ALL DAY

In addition to creating effective meetings at home and at work, you can also use these easy-but-powerful strategies for your everyday meetings with friends and strangers alike.

NAME-CALLING

One of the most important things you can do when meeting people is also the most obvious: USE THEIR NAMES. In his book, "How to Win Friends and Influence People," Dale Carnegie, the success communication guru of his time, said, "A person's name is to him or her the sweetest and most important sound in any language." Using someone's first name, especially when cultivating a warm connection, accomplishes several significant objectives in building a network, leading a team, and growing your tribe of supporters.

Here are but a few benefits to training yourself to address those around you by name:

- It shows you value them enough to remember who they are. **Don't let yourself off the hook by telling yourself you are terrible with remembering names.** Make a commitment to strengthen that mental muscle by confirming you have the name correctly and are saying it right, repeating it several times throughout a conversation, and writing it down to solidify it in your brain. If you are on the phone, jot it down and use it a few times to build rapport and connection. You can also use a creative memorization technique by linking that person's name with another person or a concept. "Mike likes to ride bikes" if he is a motorcycle enthusiast. "Lucy is as funny as Lucille Ball." "Theresa Rose is as sweet as a flower." These silly tricks are how you can solidify someone's name into your brain.

- It nudges you toward a more collaborative, service-oriented mindset as opposed to being more self-centered (literally centering oneself on his or her own responses and objectives). Demonstrating this level of presence with another is noticed and will subtly have others more committed to your efforts and the project.

- It shows that you are not a selfish dunderhead. The more you can widen your circle to bring others into the conversation by using their first names, the more you will be perceived as a nice person. And nice people make better connections, which makes for more quality output, higher sales, fewer complaints, and more engagement.

- It will get your emails read. Start every email with a personal greeting, even if it is to more than one person. (If it is a huge distribution list, use a reference to the "XYZ

Team" and then find ways to embed relevant names within the body of the email itself.) I recommend not only using a person's first name at the beginning, but also toward the end of the email. There is something far more engaging to read, "Thanks, Bob, for all you are doing to make this project a success," than "Thank you for your cooperation on this matter."

A good rule of thumb is this:

If you see someone wearing a nametag, say the name on it at least once.

I personally try to acknowledge by name every restaurant server, bartender, clerk, and doorman I encounter. You never know when having that extra connection will not only provide better service (because it does), but it also may prove incredibly important if/ when you need a helping hand.

SUPERSTRATEGY:
STORY OR SPREADSHEET

If you are like me, you have taken a personality test sometime in your life that indicates what type of person you are. Whether it's Myers-Briggs, DISC, True Colors, StrengthsFinder, or a multitude of other assessments, there are no shortages of solutions out there that help us understand ourselves and those around us. My problem with those assessments isn't that they are incorrect; it's that they are too complicated.

Complicated is bad. Complicated isn't done anymore.

Instead, I offer up a straightforward way to identify who is in the room with you or across the table from you. It's what we all know, and the simplicity makes it implementable. I categorize people into one of two primary traits: You are either a story person or a spreadsheet person. The names alone are enough for you to understand the difference.

Story people are the ones who love to provide narrative to situations. They paint pictures with their words. They are the first ones at happy hour. They are in the hallways chatting with their colleagues. They are remarkably successful in establishing and maintaining rapport with others. They flourish in marketing and sales roles. They don't mind a little chaos if it is in support of building relationships. They love people, and it shows based on the verbal and non-verbal language they use. They use a lot of commas, question marks, and exclamation points in their emails. They are awesome!

Spreadsheet people are those who just want the data. They would rather just cut to the chase and get the nuggets of information they need and move on. They like order, logic, and process. They are always on time. They bolt from the meeting as soon as it concludes. They are nowhere to be found during the optional reception. They thrive in finance, accounting, and IT. A well-written report makes them happy. They provide the foundation from which all great organizational initiatives are developed. They use periods in their emails—maybe—if they write an email longer than two words. They are awesome!

When you think about a story person versus a spreadsheet person, you can see how one can aggravate the other easily. The story person is annoyed or hurt that the spreadsheet person is cold and distant. The spreadsheet person wishes the story person would just shut up already and get to the point. The problem lies in the fact that we often communicate based on our personal style versus the style of the person with whom we are meeting.

Since this isn't a scientific assessment but rather a broad personality trait, we must rely on our observational skills in conjunction with our intuitive abilities to identify which one is in play in ourselves and others. Ideally, we are a balance of both, but for the purposes of understanding the tool, think about how the most important people in your life would categorize you as. How would your significant other, trusted co-worker, and best friend describe you? *Story* or *Spreadsheet*? Trust what others observe in you.

Now that you know what your primary tendency is, start thinking about all the people with whom you communicate. How do they talk about their personal lives? Are their emails long or short? How many friends do they have, both in real life and in the digital domain? Does everyone know them, or are they a hidden gem? Do you want to get driving directions from them? There are dozens of indicators you can keep an eye out for, so you can conduct the most effective meeting possible.

If you are a story person and you are meeting with another story person, your biggest challenge will be to get to the business at hand without wasting a bunch of time chit-chatting about nonessentials. Make sure you identify the must-haves of the meeting and get those out of the way as soon as possible. Agendas will be especially helpful to keep the two of you on track.

If you are a story person who is meeting with spreadsheet people, make sure you understand exactly what information they need, and give it to them right away. Tone down the chit-chat and thank them for taking the time to meet. Acknowledge that they are busy and get right down to business. They'll love you for it.

If you are a spreadsheet person meeting with story people, your challenge is raising your energy to their levels. Before you meet, think about one or two things you really enjoyed recently and be prepared to bring them up as small talk before the meeting begins. Take that extra swig of coffee and put on a smile to make them feel like they aren't a burden to you. Admit that you really like getting all of your ducks in a row and ask for their help in making that happen for the good of the project. Add a little extra friendliness in your emails. By amping up your own social energy, you will build deeper relationships that will serve you well in the long run.

Finally, if you are a spreadsheet person meeting with another spreadsheet person, your meetings are probably two-and-a-half minutes long. You both want to get out of there as quickly as possible with the relevant data. Start with some brief pleasantries and crank through that project punch list (or sales presentation or employee review or any other high-value meeting) as efficiently as possible. Get that agenda out and stick to it. The best way to optimize a meeting of two spreadsheets is to minimize distractions from story people. You may even want to put your agenda items at the top so at least you get the data you need at the beginning and can mentally check-out when the story people take over!

When you understand the Story or Spreadsheet SuperStrategy and can cater your personality to the person across the table from you, you will find that both your work and personal lives will get easier. You'll have fewer conflicts. You'll get things done faster. You'll make greater sales. You'll retain better talent. You'll enhance your day-to-day interactions. It's a simple and very powerful tool you can use right now to dramatically improve your meetings.

PERSON OF INCREASE

Imagine each person you run into during your day with a small plus sign or minus sign on his or her forehead. We are either plusses or minuses at any given moment. We either add to a conversation or take away from it. We either optimize a situation or undercut it. When we are in the store and impatiently grumble at the overwhelmed cashier, we are making the situation worse, not better. When we are in a meeting and we respond to someone's idea with, "We've already tried that, and it didn't work", we are detracting from the discussion instead of fostering a collaborative, innovative environment. When we choose to put our own interests ahead of others, we are fundamentally robbing our counterparts of the opportunity to have their needs met as well.

Have an eye toward finding new ways to increase profits and make your organization more efficient. When you are in a meeting, regardless if you are hosting it or not, be on the lookout for ways in which the process can be improved. Without undercutting anyone's authority or influence, make a note of innovative ways that meetings and other communications can be enhanced and then *offer to drive the implementation.*

That's the power of being a person of increase. It isn't enough to know how to make something bigger, better, or more profitable;

one must also have a sense of service to make the enhancement come to fruition. We don't have to do it all by ourselves, but we need to take ownership of the tactical aspects of completion.

Nobody likes a know-it-all who is also a do-nothing.

If you see a way to make something better, name it and then offer to help.

This strategy is one I have taken extremely seriously in my own life, both professionally and personally. Every single day as part of my manifestation process, I describe how I am going to accomplish my big visions by "being a person of increase in every exchange." I originally heard of this concept many years ago when I participated in a life coaching program by Mary Morissey, whom I highly recommend. Just like campers and hikers who are advised to "leave the land better than how you found it", so too can we utilize this principle in every transaction, every day. Here are a few examples of how you can become a legendary person of increase:

- When you are in a retail store, instead of surfing on your phone, look the cashier in the eyes and say, "Thank you, (Name)!"

- Leave a generous tip for that scrappy server who is doing her best.

- Clean up the conference room of extra papers and other trash that accumulated throughout your meeting.

- Sort the project action item list the way the team prefers it before sending it out.

- Start every networking conversation with a genuine offer to help and before that conversation ends, identify specific suggestions on how you could help.

- Say "Thank you" as much as you possibly can to every single person who helps you in any way, from the volunteers who are sprucing up the neighborhood in the spring to the tired cleaning person who is wiping the sinks in the airport restroom.

By becoming a person of increase in every exchange, you broadcast to the world that you are a solution-provider, not a problem-creator. When you genuinely become a bright light for everyone you meet, the Universe begins to conspire in your favor. It starts to put the perfect person in your orbit who will help you reach your goals. Thanks to the Law of Reciprocity, it will nudge others to want to help you in any way they can. And most importantly, you will be able to sleep well at night, knowing that in a very difficult and challenging new world, you are a bringer of goodness, not of bitterness. Lastly, as a bonus, your body will run better and last longer.

Now more than ever, the world needs more people who are committed to adding to the collective goodness versus taking away from it.

Civility training is on the rise, and for good reason. (One could argue that civility training should be a requirement before anyone runs for political office. Just sayin'.) People are just not being *nice* anymore. They aren't listening, aren't showing respect to those who hold different views than themselves, and they find it perfectly acceptable to only do what *they* want to do. This is causing significant divisiveness in our organizations and in our world. The news is full of descriptions of people suffering from the repercussions of bullying and harassment. We need to combat this divide one smile, acknowledgement, and thank you at a time.

By bringing greater focus and awareness to our meetings at home, at work, and in our communities, we are paving the pathways to success while also contributing to a more compassionate, charitable, and civil society. Mindful, effective discussions are critical, as all great accomplishments are a group effort. Our visions become a reality when we create in conscious collaboration.

SELF-REFLECTION: **MEETINGS**

What are your strengths in this focus area?

_____

_____

_____

_____

What are your opportunities for growth?

_____

_____

_____

_____

What specific life experiences came up for you as you read
through this chapter? What was the impact to you personally
and professionally?

_____

_____

_____

_____

How would improving your activity and awareness in this focus area help you reach your goals?

_____

_____

_____

_____

What are the strategies that resonated with you the most?

- **House Meeting Logistics**
- **Complete Conversations**
- **Embracing Emotion**
- **Money Value of Time**
- **Unified Arrival**
- **Mindful Meeting Mastery**
- **Name-calling**
- **Story or Spreadsheet (SuperStrategy)**
- **Person of Increase**

What is one action you will take to increase your performance in this area, and by when will you do it?

_____

_____

_____

_____

CHAPTER 7

MENTORS & MASTERMINDS

....

No matter how smart, talented, or driven we are, we cannot manifest our life vision by ourselves. Every last one of us needs help, at least every once in a while. We need the way-show-ers, the door-openers, the educators, the cautionary tale-tellers, and the wheel-greasers to get us there. Sometimes those teachers and supporters come in the form of formal mentors, and other times they are simply informal providers of priceless wisdom.

If you are looking to enhance your organization's reputation, step into a more challenging role, or become the best at what you do, then getting a mentor is an essential step. Mentors are people who are leaders in your field. They make the money you want to make, hobnob with other sensational leaders, and seem to have it all figured out. Do you personally know these people, and do they know you?

Your mentors should be people who are accomplished at what you want to be doing. They know the terrain like the backs of their hands. They understand the processes, pitfalls, and politics. They are your models for future strategies, so make sure you are learning from the best.

How do you get a mentor? The answer is unique for each person. It's almost like asking, "How do I find a partner?" It's preparation, chemistry, and luck that will open the right doors. Make sure you are paying attention to the Cosmic Noogies that may be leading you to the perfect person. Your job is to be ready when opportunities organically present themselves.

What's not okay is to selfishly pounce on your industry high performers by saying, "Will you be my mentor?" at the very first opportunity. Earn the right to ask for mentorship by demonstrating your competency and commitment over a span of time. Contribute to causes or projects for which they are passionate. When the time comes, describe exactly what type of assistance you are looking for and what you will do in exchange for their valuable time.

Masterminds are also incredibly powerful collaborations that can take your successes to the stratosphere. I originally heard of the concept of a mastermind group when I read Mom's favorite book, "Think and Grow Rich". A mastermind is a trusted group of colleagues or other individuals who have a shared interest in expanding their individual successes and are committed to harnessing their collective energy to make them a reality. They do this by supporting each other's vision with honest feedback, insights, and encouragement.

My performance, impact, and income as a speaker exploded when I began to participate in formal mastermind groups and their younger sibling, the accountability partnership. You get to hear from different perspectives, elicit great ideas, and create an exciting win-for-everyone mentality that makes the entire group better. (The idea for this book originally began as a discussion item with my mastermind group around a conference room table in Dallas.)

Make sure you choose the right people when establishing a mastermind. You don't want to be the only one who knows anything. There should be people who are smarter, better, and more talented than you are, otherwise your mastermind gatherings may get out of balance. You may find yourself dispensing free advice without receiving anything in return. It will drain you and quickly become a net-negative experience. Yes, it is a commitment to engage in a formal group relationship, especially if your mastermind members are not local and you require occasional face-to-face retreats. However, like everything, it is an investment. The more time you put into it, the more you will get out of it.

Let's dive into how you can leverage mentors and masterminds to create greater impact at home, at work, and in the community.

AT HOME

Sometimes we need to be the mentors and teachers for our team at home. There are best practices you can employ that will maximize the likelihood that your team (your significant other, your children, your housemates, and anyone else with whom you have a reciprocal personal relationship) will do what you need them to do to improve the overall quality of your surroundings and connections.

GO FORTH AND DELEGATE

One of the best strategies you can employ as a home mentor is mastering the art of delegation. When you empower your home team, you'll have fewer tasks on your plate while reducing your stress levels.

When you are teaching a new activity to people in your home—let's say doing laundry or taking the garbage out, for example—you'll want to be very specific about what you want them to do. (Laundry is a multi-phase process; it doesn't just involve throwing clothes in the washer, pouring detergent, and turning the knobs.) Show them how you do it and what important aspects are "must haves". Let them know you don't expect them to be as good at it as you are, at least not at the beginning. You don't want to hear, "Yes, but I don't do it as well as you do!" as an excuse that results in you doing everything. You may be a cooking dynamo, but that should not preclude your significant other from stepping up to the plate—literally and figuratively—every once in a while.

Don't let the specter of perfection get in the way of leveraging your home team.

You'll always be better at performing any task you regularly perform than others are. You've done them longer. Perfect is not the goal when reallocating responsibilities across all members of the household. I used to tell my daughter that if she scrubs the toilet 70% as well as I do, then that is A-OK with me.

PICK YOUR VICTORIES

In the interest of promoting peace in the household, consider choosing which areas you'll mentor someone for improvement. Choose those aspects of household upkeep that truly make a substantive difference in the long-term benefit of all involved. I am a self-identified neat freak, and it drove me absolutely crazy to enter my child's post-apocalypse room. Each visit to my daughter's room required a steely reserve and haz-mat suit. She'd leave clothes all over the floor, empty junk food wrappers wherever she chose, and generally created a mine field of obstacles that would prohibit even the heartiest adventurer from entering the perimeter without calling for emergency backup. (I'm pretty sure she is my offspring, but this makes me wonder if there was a mix-up in the hospital nursery.)

For years I'd beg, plead, get angry, and spend an inordinate amount of time and energy on expensive organizational tools, only to be categorically ignored until drastic measures were taken (taking her cell phone away, which if you ask my daughter, is a fate worse than death). It was a battle of wills every single day. I once consulted with a master Feng Shui practitioner on what I could do to address the nightmare that is my teenage daughter's room. Her response was simple and highly effective: "Close the door."

Unless you want to live in seclusion on a pristine mountaintop, you will run into those territories that trigger defensiveness and agitation because of your cohabitants' choices. Choose your battles carefully, whether it's putting the toilet seat up (or down), wiping down the counter *and stove* after cooking spaghetti, or putting the mail in the basket versus on the table. Which ones are simply too egregious for you to ignore, and which are the ones you can let slide? Be firm on the ones that are "must-haves" and find ways to genuinely accept the reality that you will not be 100% satisfied with items lower on the priority scale. I like to use every time my daughter does something bone-headed as an opportunity to practice gratitude that she is in my life rather than letting it burn a hole in my stomach from upset. Life is too short to constantly worry or nag your loved ones to put the toilet paper on correctly—which is clearly forward facing, as God meant it to be. When triggered with those niggling items, forego being the mentor who knows all, opting for flexibility and gratitude instead. It will promote peace and preserve the relationship.

SPECIFICS OVER SILENCE

If you find an opportunity to improve the environment in your home, don't assume that your silence will be an effective communication vehicle. When it comes to resolving conflict, silence is never the solution; specifics are. Be gentle but direct. Tell the people exactly what you are hoping to have happen and *why*. Ask them what they think of your suggestion and see if they are of the same mind. Show them what would be a better solution for all involved.

An executive coaching client of mine struggled with a spouse who didn't contribute to household responsibilities, including meal preparation. This was a sore spot for her, as she came home exhausted from an intense day at work. He expected her to provide dinner—every single night, for years. She was growing increasingly resentful and was worried about the future of her relationship. Her response was to shut down. Of course, her spouse had no idea what the problem was and how his actions (or inactions) fueled her anger.

I suggested she purchase a pressure cooker, pick out a recipe that her entire family would love, and acquire the necessary ingredients. She specifically asked to schedule a "cooking date" with her honey on a weekend when they would walk through the entire process together (with Cabernets in hand). At dinner, she said how much it would mean to her if he could cook one meal a week. He committed to doing it, especially if it meant a happier wife! He just needed specific instructions that would make him successful. It wasn't enough for her to say, "Make dinner once in a while!" She needed to walk through the process with him. By doing so, it gave him the confidence he needed to tackle an area that previously gave him anxiety.

Yes, maintaining a mindful home life takes effort on everyone's part. However, it is an investment of time that is well worth having. Chapter 10 further explores how your environment impacts your performance. Whether it is sharing the duties of cooking, cleaning, shopping, or financial management, it really does take everyone in the village to help create a home.

AT WORK

....

I am blessed to not only know but also be great friends with one of the leaders in my field of professional speaking, Connie Podesta. Connie is my mentor and a rockstar ninja who has helped me up my game as a keynote speaker onstage and off. She has taught me more over mimosas and late-night texts than I have learned from all the bestselling business books, expensive conferences, and exclusive coaching programs combined.

When you establish a relationship with mentors, genuinely thank them for their generosity of time and attention. Send them a thoughtful card after a particularly helpful session. Give them heartfelt kudos on social media or through inter-office communications. Find tactful ways to show them how much you truly honor and appreciate their contributions to your growth and development.

When you are ready to grow your brand or business, sometimes the best thing you can do is shift your focus from learning new information from endless "expert" resources to **doing a deep-dive with one mentor who truly knows your industry from the inside out.**

EARN BEFORE THE ASK

Oftentimes a professional mentor has several high-value relation-ships that could substantially improve your career path or earn you more money. It is tempting to immediately ask them for an intro-duction to that Big Whale Client or put in a good word with the top brass. *Don't do it.* Instead, keep finding ways to make deposits into your relationship bank account. Be singularly focused on learning and giving back to the mentors who help you. Once you have firmly established a solid history of reciprocity, then and only then should you ask for one strategically-relevant favor. But if you are being a mindful mentee, chances are you won't even have to make that ask. Nine times out of ten, the right mentor will be on the lookout for ways to help you before you even make a request. You want that fabulous moment when they open the doors to new opportunities to be one they naturally want to do because of your dedication and talent, not because you are a pest.

DO WHAT YOUR MENTORS SAY

There are four steps you can take to optimally leverage your mentorship: 1) Learn, 2) Plan, 3) Commit, and 4) Execute.

Learn

While it is tempting to impress your business gurus just as they have impressed you, don't try to dazzle them with all of your vast knowledge, experience, and insight. Listen to them and soak in every bit of wisdom, criticism, and advice they give. You are the learner; they are the teacher.

Watch how they conduct themselves in meetings, at presentations, over email, with clients, on the road, and over the telephone. What do they wear? How do they show up? What types of questions do they ask? How do they execute daily activities? How are their emails written? Some of the greatest lessons you will learn will come from observation of the smallest details.

The more you deeply listen, the shorter your learning curve will be.

Plan

Immediately put a plan in place to take action on your mentors' suggestions when they give you advice on how to grow your business or improve your skill set. Pull all the resources together to properly and fully execute your new direction. Seek out additional support to help you organize your approach and streamline any processes.

Commit

It's time to assign dates to completion once you have put deliberate thought into your approach and solidify your plan. Revisit the *Who's Going to Do What by When* strategy (as discussed in Chapter 5) to nail down specifics. Share your commitment dates with your mentor. Take a firm stance that you will accomplish your goal. ("Do or do not; there is no try."–Yoda) Your mentor will be impressed by your firm commitment and will likely offer even more assistance when appropriate.

Execute

Once your plan is in place and you have made a firm commitment to complete, take action ASAP. Get on it. Do not delay. Don't let fear make you second-guess their advice. Take those action steps quickly and circle back with your mentors right away to let them know you've moved forward based on their helpful counsel. They will see that you mean business and will give you more and more valuable recommendations.

Always have your next big goal specifically identified when you are working with mentors or are in a mastermind group. Be clear in what you are going to create and by when. Choose a tangible goal that is realistic but a stretch and share it with the group. Whether it's a sales goal, an educational credential, or even reading a certain book, say you'll do it and then do it. Know your Big Goal at any given time and write it down on a piece of paper or post-it note you will easily see every single day. Keep it top-of-mind so you can work diligently toward accomplishing it. Better yet, incorporate it into your Statement of Intention as discussed in Chapter 5 to hyper-focus on its inevitability.

Mentorship isn't a one-way street.

The longest-lasting, most successful mentorships are give-and-take relationships where the mentors are rewarded for their selfless contributions to your success. Make it your mission to help your mentors out whenever you possibly can, personally and professionally. Jump on it when you spot an opportunity to make a beneficial connection or referral. Step up to volunteer if they need assistance for a meeting or special event. Coordinate a task force that is important to them. Donate to their children's cookie drive. Do whatever you can to return the favor, as long as you aren't coming across as an annoying brown-noser.

MASTERMIND MECHANICS

There are plenty of resources online that share how to facilitate a mastermind. While there aren't any hard and fast rules, here are some best practices that I find to be very effective.

First, decide on logistics. Where will the meeting be held? Is it face-to-face, or do you need to meet virtually? Face-to-face is obviously preferred, given that you can build deeper relationships when you have plenty of time with each other. Bear in mind where everyone is coming from and assign a location that is as convenient as possible for every participant. Make sure you allow for travel delays. You don't want to start your mastermind until every single member has safely arrived and has acclimated to the environment.

Second, it is helpful to create plenty of social time before, during, and after the intensity of your mastermind meeting. The whole idea of a mastermind is to honestly share your visions and challenges in order to move through resistance and inertia. The meeting itself can be mentally and emotionally demanding. Build in fun time (with or without adult beverages!) that will balance out the energy.

Third, craft an agenda with strict timeframes that will allow each person to share their most important challenges and questions and receive sufficient feedback for each. Ensure that each person gets an equal amount of time (20-60 minutes are typical timeframes) and encourage them not to waste their precious minutes on exposition or background. If there is information that is pertinent for the rest of the participants to know, e.g. reviewing a website, watching a video, or reading a document, then have those actions assigned as pre-work. Identify one person as timekeeper to stay on track. Consider audio recording each portion so participants don't have to spend any extra energy taking notes and can be fully present with the feedback they receive. Establish ground rules about what will and won't be discussed and how feedback will be given.

Make sure everyone feels safe and encouraged to give and receive totally honest feedback.

Finally, a high-performance mastermind is only as good as the follow-through. Encourage everyone to identify one or two mission-critical actions they *will* take as a result of the mastermind, and when they will be completed. Do this before each person's allotted timeframe is finished. Create a Closed Facebook group or other electronic forum to encourage accountability and connection in between your meetings. When powerful, smart, focused, and dedicated people harness their collective energy and wisdom, big dreams become big realities.

ALL DAY

Here are a few strategies and mindsets that will dramatically amplify the positive results of your mentorships and masterminds both professionally and personally.

SUPERSTRATEGY:
GUT-PUNCH OF TRUTH

Many of us have grown up in a judgment-oriented learning environment. We are graded on our performance, our attitudes, and our efforts from a very young age, and oftentimes we correlate those grades with our intrinsic value as people. If we are "A" students, we are good. If we make mistakes, we are bad. This type of binary, good-versus-bad evaluation system can have a negative, long-term impact on our personal and professional development because of our discomfort with criticism. This can be a major inhibitor to our growth as leaders and high performers. I struggled with this for many years, as evidenced by reviewing old report cards and performance evaluations, all of which would say that my biggest challenge was that I "didn't take criticism well". (What do they know anyway? Kidding.)

If you really want to supercharge your performance in your career and life, surround yourself with successful people who will be brutally honest about the very things you are most sensitive to. I went years in my speaking business following advice from countless coaches and colleagues who told me to keep going down a certain path with my brand and offering, never having the courage to tell me that I was woefully tone-deaf to what the marketplace was actually willing to pay for. Furthermore, people are often comfortable with providing feedback that is either positive or gently hints at subtle tweaks you can make around the periphery.

It doesn't help you to have mentors and masterminds who are afraid to tell you what you really need to hear.

My speaking career catapulted when I got a mentor who was not afraid to tell me the pure unadulterated, sometimes-ugly truth about my professional shortcomings. As a legend in the speaking business, Connie took me under her wing to show me the ropes of how to be a top-tier keynote speaker. From the very first conversation we had, she told me exactly why I wasn't creating the kind of business that was worthy of me. As our relationship matured and deepened, her feedback became, shall we say, more pointed than ever. She'd tell me things that could improve my performance that no one ever would have said, things like "you need to modulate your energy; you are making the audience tired," or "that photo shouldn't be on your website because you don't look good in it" or "you won't be able to sell to corporate audiences with what you are offering now". WOW. Those things were hard to hear. But she was absolutely right.

Every time I have a mentoring session with Connie, she shares some major nugget of insight that substantively improves my business, whether it's stage performance, sales negotiation, or client management. By receiving this priceless wisdom from a bona fide superstar, the only price I must pay is the initial Gut-punch of Truth. The sting my ego initially feels is nothing compared to what I get in return. I just steel myself for the blow, know it will happen, and feel grateful for the wisdom contained within it.

Find teachers who will tell you what others won't. Encourage them to speak the unspeakable. Tell them to take off the kid gloves and tell you what you need to hear. You may not like it at first, but if you have the courage and confidence to look beyond the ouch and implement what they suggest, you will be head and shoulders above your competition. Tighten those gut muscles!

PERSONAL ADVISORY BOARD

No matter how smart you are or how much experience you have, there is value to having a formalized group of people who know you, love you, and support you to give you feedback and ideas for improvement in all major areas of your life. Whether it's investing in that expensive health improvement package, deciding on a time-frame to make a major pivot in your career, or trekking across the countryside on an outward-bound excursion, consider creating a Personal Advisory Board from a variety of backgrounds who can give you their two cents.

Oftentimes an outside person can see beyond the emotional aspects of a decision to give insight on impacts you may not be considering, whether they are physical, economic, relational, or any other hidden nuance that your passion may have made you blind to. Your Personal Advisory Board can serve as a valued second opinion who will help you see opportunities that are hidden to you, or be the voice of reason when something isn't in alignment with your stated vision and mission.

Create a network of powerful advocates who are deeply committed to supporting you. Mindfully cultivate the key relationships in your life. Just make sure you don't select someone who is unable to be objective. Identify a few smart people you trust and who also have the personal integrity to push back when appropriate. You don't need any more yes-men/women in your life.

You need strong, smart, supportive people who will call attention to your blind spots and share whole new possibilities that you never even imagined.

Take a moment now to jot down a half-dozen people who you think would be perfect as members of your Personal Advisory Board. Think about how you'd like to engage them. And then pick up the phone.

GAME FOOTAGE

Professional athletes watch the latest game footage in order to dissect what went right with their performances and what could be improved upon. They painstakingly review the missteps so they can learn from them, course-correct, and improve next time. It takes a strong will to endure watching your mistakes (and having others watch them), but it is a key aspect of being a top performer.

As a speaker, the best way for me to improve is to watch my game footage—the video from a presentation. Let me tell you, this exercise is not for the faint of heart. Watching oneself onstage brings with it a whole level of self-awareness that tweaks all kinds of insecurities. When I watch video of me performing, a litany of thoughts initially floods my mind:

- "I look like Quasimodo in rhinestones!"

- "Do I really sound that annoying?"

- "What on earth am I doing with my face?"

- "I can't even believe I said that in front of a room full of people."

The first time I watch, suffice it to say there is a fair amount of cringing, cussing, and averting my eyes. However, the second viewing allows me to see fewer Quasimodo moments and more of the inspiring ones. By the third viewing, I have (almost) let go of the cosmetic or surface imperfections and embraced the deeper lessons and takeaways of the footage.

Even if you aren't a speaker, you can use the game footage strategy to improve your performance. If you are a leader, record yourself facilitating some of your meetings or making presentations; review your performance, keeping a watchful eye for areas of improvement or other opportunities to refine your message and presence. Do you have any nervous tics you weren't even aware of (such as using filler words like Umms, Uhs, Likes, Sort of's, You know's)? Are you speaking too quickly or harshly? Are you smiling or frowning? Do you solicit involvement from everyone or just your favorite go-to people? Is there a topic you skated through because you aren't as confident with it?

If you are in sales, record one or more of your voicemail messages or phone calls with your prospects. Is your voice warm and inviting, or does it come across as sales-schmoozy? Do you make it about them right away, or do you talk too much about yourself? Do you talk too fast because of nerves? Did you really listen and respond accordingly, or did you plow forward with your canned pitch, regardless of what they were saying? Did you ask for a specific call to action, or did you leave it open for them to ignore you?

If you are an individual contributor, review the written game footage contained in your Sent file.

Review some older emails or reports. What kind of language are you using? Are you using positive, team-oriented verbiage, or do you write more self-serving language? Do you request or demand? Would a new employee want to work with you or help you? Do you get to the point right away, or do you waste their time with a lot of unnecessary blah-blah-blah?

Regularly review how you are presenting yourself to your colleagues and customers in order to identify areas of focus that will improve your skills and reputation. Ask your mentor and mastermind team to review your footage and let you know what they think. (Encourage the Gut-punch of Truth!) Have the fortitude to clearly see how you are being perceived by others so you can make necessary modifications.

Remember, awareness plus action equals improvement.

By humbly learning from masters in your industry, you will set yourself up to be the next generation of game-changing, leaderboard-topping, buzz-creating leaders who naturally create the careers that future leaders will desire. When that eventually happens, don't forget that special mentor and mastermind group who helped get you there and do them proud by reaching out to help that earnest newbie who was once like you.

SELF-REFLECTION:
MENTORS & MASTERMINDS

What are your strengths in this focus area?

_____

_____

_____

_____

What are your opportunities for growth?

_____

_____

_____

_____

What specific life experiences came up for you as you read through this chapter? What was the impact to you personally and professionally?

_____

_____

_____

_____

How would improving your activity and awareness in this focus area help you reach your goals?

_____

_____

_____

_____

What are the strategies that resonated with you the most?

- **Go Forth and Delegate**
- **Pick Your Victories**
- **Specifics Over Silence**
- **Earn Before the Ask**
- **Do What Your Mentors Say**
- **Mastermind Mechanics**
- **Gut-punch of Truth (SuperStrategy)**
- **Personal Advisory Board**
- **Game Footage**

What is one action you will take to increase your performance in this area, and by when will you do it?

_____

_____

_____

_____

CHAPTER 8

MESSAGES

....

Words matter. They are the way we take what is in our heads and hearts and translate it for others to receive, assimilate, and take action upon—or not. When our messages are weak, negative, or incomplete, they create a barrier to understanding that wastes time, costs money, and erodes relationships.

How we say something in verbal or written form is just as important as *what* we say.

Imagine yourself in a meeting. Your boss calls you out in front of everyone by saying, "You really screwed this up, and now all of us have to deal with cleaning up your mess." How does that make you feel? How do you think it makes others feel? How long does that careless communication stay with you? What long-term damage does it do to your relationship with your boss?

Or maybe your boss does the opposite. She only calls you when she needs something or is in the middle of an organizational fire-drill. You never get quality time with her to talk through your progress, priorities, and problems. This is equally damaging to you and your upward trajectory. Gallup did a study on employee engagement and satisfaction that showed one in two employees left a job to *get away from the manager*. Employees don't leave because they want more money; they leave because they don't like their boss.[11]

Messages can come in a variety of formats: face-to-face conversations, presentations, telephone calls, emails, reports, proposals, business forms, and even texts.

Every word you write and speak is evaluated by the recipient not only for clarity, correctness and comprehension, but also for tone.

The messages you share tell the world the kind of person you are. Are you open or close-minded? Helpful or selfish? Accountable or blaming? Friendly or aloof? Calm or stressed? Optimistic or pessimistic? A leader or a follower? A solution-provider or a problem-causer? Every single time you send a message, you get to decide how you are perceived by those in your orbit.

AT HOME

....

When our communications at home are healthy, our stress decreases and we are much more able to focus on priorities that serve our long-term health and balance.

POLARITY POTHOLES

How many times have you found yourself saying, "You *always* make me do X" or "You *never* do Y"? That type of polarizing language, especially when used in difficult discussions—always/never, black/white—often undercuts your message because the recipients are too busy defending themselves instead of truly listening. While we do it at work as well—"You are always late", "He never does his fair share of the project work", "She never volunteers to help with our team activities"—it tends to be especially present at home with those closest to us.

Maybe it's because we are tired when we get home from a long day at work, or maybe we just have allowed ourselves to get overly comfortable when communicating with our loved ones.

Regardless of the reason, using rigid, inflexible language that paints someone in a corner can do major damage. When people hear polarizing language directed toward them, they immediately seek out an example where that statement is false. "Oh yeah? Just the other day I helped you with the dishes!" Or "I took you out for dinner three times last month!" Then the discussion devolves into back-and-forth splitting of hairs instead of really dealing with the underlying issue.

Keep a watchful eye on the language you use to ensure you aren't unnecessarily making it harder to connect and understand each other. By using precise language that is more fact-based, you will end up getting a lot more accomplished while building stronger bonds.

I OVER YOU

In relationships it is so easy to identify the shortcomings of the other person. Whenever we find ourselves in conflict, we often resort to You-based language:

- "You don't do enough around the house."

- "You don't support me."

- "You are constantly complaining about everything I do."

These are common refrains in domestic or personal exchanges. Yes, it may feel briefly emotionally satisfying to lash out at someone who has caused you pain or frustration, but it is ultimately not the kind of messaging that brings about long-term success and growth.

The next time you need to have a difficult conversation, consider coming only from *your* point of view. Own your feelings and expectations while not projecting onto the other person. "I am feeling very overwhelmed by the domestic duties in addition to my workload" is so much healthier than barking out, "You don't do enough around the house". Or, "I am really needing some extra support right now as I am working through a lot of uncertainty with my job" shows a level of vulnerability that opens up people's hearts as opposed to accusing them of neglect when you say, "You are never there for me". If you are feeling attacked or judged by another, boldly own those feelings ("I have been upset because I feel like I am disappointing you") instead of placing the focus on their shortcomings ("You are constantly complaining about everything I do").

The softer (and clearer) we can make our messages, the further we will go toward genuine communication and connection.

People will stop putting up defenses and start truly listening to what we have to say.

YES, AND

I perform improvisational comedy. When a performer responds negatively to someone's declaration (Performer #1: "I hate waiting in line at the grocery store." Performer #2: "We aren't at the grocery store; we're at the mall!"), it is a sure-fire way to halt the scene in its tracks. The two players are on two different wavelengths, and trust is eroded. The same holds true when we are in dialogue with our families, friends, and professional colleagues. Too often we jump to "no" instead of acknowledging the other person's standpoint and then building upon it to grow the interaction.

When my daughter was little, I used to call her Princess YesBut. I would say, "Emma, it's time for you to clean your room," to which she would reply, "Yes, but ... I'm playing with my toys now." Everything I would ask her to do, she would respond with "Yes, but ..." People don't listen to anything after they hear the word "but". It's all noise.

One of the core tenets that an improvisor learns right away is the concept of "Yes, and". It is a simple but critical component of a successful scene between two people. Train yourself to replace that "but" with an "and". You'll see the scenes of your life will become a lot more productive. "Yes, and" invites you to automatically accept what is presented to you from others, acknowledging their truths, and encourages you to advance and expand on what is presented. For example, if your child wants to go shopping for the latest gadget, instead of immediately saying no, consider saying, "Yes, I totally get that you want that new device. It does seem pretty fantastic. And, I am not comfortable buying it for you because it is much more expensive than our budget allows. However, what do you think about putting together a plan where you can pay for half?"

By embodying a "Yes, and" communication approach, you are opening the doors to collaboration and innovation you never would have thought of without advancing the dialogue in a positive, mutually-supportive way.

AT WORK

Messages at work are the basis of our performance. When we create mindful, empowering, and growth-oriented messaging, our success skyrockets and our reputation is enhanced.

DELIGHTFUL NETWORKING

Imagine you are in sales and are at a networking event or having a virtual coffee with a new prospect. You want to build the strongest bond possible in the quickest amount of time. You immediately attempt to dazzle your future buyers with how awesome you are, paying paltry lip-service to the customer. It's one of the most challenging aspects of being in sales. With the pressures for quotas, commissions, and contracts, it's easy to entrench oneself in the mindset of "close the deal!" But deals cannot be closed if the partnership of "we" hasn't been established yet, and "we" can't be established until the "you" in the equation is honored.

I used to hate networking. It felt so artificial and forced. Overzealous participants throwing their business cards at you (and me in return) without so much as a how-do-you-do. That kind of networking never works. How many times have you come home after a networking event with a stack of business cards, only to throw them out? Guess what? Your prospects are doing the same thing.

Unless you employ the Delightful Networking strategy.

In order to be successful, you must put the "light" in Delightful Networking. That means adopting a gentle approach, one that doesn't feel sales-y. When I connect with someone at an event, my only goal is to learn something interesting about them, discover why they are there, and what I can do to help them in some way either personally or professionally. I'm constantly on the lookout for ways I can provide support and make another feel good. That may be as simple as saying "Great tie!" to a man standing in the bar line, to "I love your outfit!" to a woman in the ladies' lounge. Have fun at the event with no goal of gathering business cards. Be charming.

Exude enthusiasm.

And when you finally connect to further the conversation, remember what got you there in the first place.

When I have my virtual coffees with people I meet networking, I automatically do research on them online to learn more about their background so I can ask them about it when we speak. I ask a ton of questions and give my assistance when I can (e.g. how to write a book, presentation best practices, sales techniques that work, etc.) And then, here's the key, I'll try to end the conversation *before* I tell them anything about me. After I have spent the past fifteen to thirty minutes being genuinely interested in their businesses and helpful to them in some meaningful way, I'll be perfectly willing to walk away. However, the Law of Reciprocity won't allow that to happen, and they will feel compelled to ask me about my career as a speaker.

Bingo. Paydirt.

I then get to tell them a little bit about what I do, but I still don't ask for anything. I just matter-of-factly tell them what I do and then bring the attention back to them. They will eventually push to find ways to give me assistance just like I gave them. It is a light approach to networking that takes all of the smarmy salesiness out of it and only allows your best, most helpful, most delightful self to emerge. And that version of yourself makes the strongest possible impression.

THOUGHT-FULL EMAILS

When was the last time you wrote a letter you actually mailed from the post office? How about writing a memo? Still using the fax machine? Thanks to technological advancements, those forms of communication have largely gone the way of the VCR. Email is now the primary way through which we communicate at work. It has become the standard method of disseminating information among our colleagues, supervisors, customers, and prospects. Yet, one of the most common complaints is that no one *reads* our emails anymore. Many of us receive dozens if not hundreds of emails a day. How can we create meaningful, profitable connections with our co-workers and customers that will make them click the Enter key instead of Delete?

It's a simple solution, but one most people do not do. We need to write for our recipients, not ourselves. Write electronic communications that are thoughtful of the people in the "To" field instead of tap-tap-tapping away at our message stream-of-consciousness style in order to crank through as much work as possible. I get it; writing mindfully takes longer than just spewing out what is in our heads. One of my favorite quotes is from French philosopher Blaise Pascal: *"I have made this longer than usual because I have not had time to make it shorter."*

I have often coached professionals on the most effective methods of business writing and email communications as part of my work as a speaker and consultant. Here are a few things to consider when you open up that next email window to relay your important message:

- Is your "Subject" field compelling enough to avoid the insta-delete? Is it 50 characters or less so the recipient can read the gist of the email before opening it? Have you written it in a way that conveys exactly what's in the message, or have you made an email faux-pas such as writing a sentence ("We need to talk about project X ..."), being vague ("A few issues" or "Hi there"), being boring or self-serving ("Let me introduce you to our product"), or worse yet, *nothing?*

Your subject line is the single most important piece of writing you'll do via email.

If you don't pass the Enter-Over-Delete test, then your performance will plummet because you'll be wasting precious time following up on unread emails. Write one subject in each email, using a subject description that tells what it's about, e.g. "Confirming Lunch at Noon on Wed. 5/12". You will help your recipients manage their own time by doing so, and they will be far more likely to want to partner with you, both online and off.

- Have you said hello before diving into your message? No one wants to be barked at, and this includes email communication as well. People read emails as if they are listening to you speak. As such, greet them as you would if you would be speaking with them in person. Use the person's first name (or list the names of a few people on this list or identify the team somehow) so they know you took the time to think of *them*. If this is not a recurring message, authentically say something complimentary or pleasant to warm them up to the rest of your message ("Congrats on rocking it at the board meeting yesterday!")

- Make the message about them, not you. If your email is peppered with "I want ... " and "I need ... ", they will tune out. Instead, look at your I-to-You ratio and make sure you are giving them a reason to *want* to read through your note and take action. If you don't, your message will never get the eyeballs you desire.

- Don't write long, rambling paragraphs that show you haven't thought through what you actually *want* from them. Tell them up front what the purpose of the email is and what action, if any, you want them to take. The supplemental information can be included later on in the email. Don't bury the lead by making your reader slog through seven scrolls before getting to the meat; I promise you, if you make it hard for them to decipher what the point of your email is, they will have already jumped ship long ago and moved on to something less taxing.

- Use formatting to your advantage. Break up the information into intuitive chunks with paragraphs or bulleted lists. Use color judiciously to highlight dates (purple), people's names (blue), and data (green).

Write critical sentences or fragments in BOLD font or color highlighter to draw greater attention to what they really need to read.

We all know people aren't *really* reading the entire email anyway; they are scanning. Make it easy for them.

- Write like you speak. Don't suddenly become a buttoned-up business automaton over email simply because it's written communication. Be you. Let your voice jump off the screen. You'll make a bigger impact.

Writing mindful emails takes extra time and effort. You can't just crank out whatever comes to your mind and hit send. Every single line you write should be thoughtful and compel your recipients to read more. Always proofread your emails. You'll catch embarrassing typos before they leave your keyboard.

SPEWER VS. DOER

Facebook used to just be for our family and friends, people we *actually* knew. Those days are long gone, and it is now used by hiring managers and buyers all the time to vet you before they have even contacted you.

What does your digital footprint say about you? Are you a Spewer—someone who complains about work, weather, politics, stress, technology, and co-workers? Or are you a Doer—someone who enthusiastically shares amazing things you have done to rock it at work, help others, and enjoy life? It's a simple concept but so many of us fall victim to thinking that those checking us out on Facebook or other social media agree with us. They don't. Many of them hold directly opposing views and will not think twice about putting you in the "No" pile if they think you are a whiner or will stir up trouble.

You may be thinking, "Hey, I can express myself in whatever way I want to on my own time and on my own social media page!" You are absolutely right. You can. But know that if you decide to share your biases, insecurities, polarizing political views, or negativity, people *will* judge you and you *will* experience the repercussions of your choice. You may get passed up for the job you are seeking. You may not close the big deal you have been counting on. You may alienate the people you rely upon to play nice with you at work and in your personal life.

If you really want to have an unfiltered outlet for your more polarizing side, create a fake profile and share away. Or call friends and vent to them about the injustices you are experiencing. Just know that everything you publicly post can and will be evaluated by influential people you don't even know. They will form an opinion of the kind of person you are based on what they see of you online. Be circumspect about what you share in today's environment of concerns about identity theft and selling your data.

If you want to up-level your career, be a Doer, not a Spewer.

ALL DAY

....

We don't live in a vacuum; our lives are inextricably linked to those in our homes, at our workplaces, and throughout our daily journeys. We are all a part of a larger whole—humanity—and the more we send messages that acknowledge and honor others, the more successful and content we will be.

THE MIDDLE WAY

Knowing the difference between right and wrong was easy when I was growing up. You inherently knew what right behavior was (ethical, honest, compassionate, selfless) and everyone relied on a single set of facts (the *actual* ones, not the alternative ones) to decide if something was wrong or not.

The world is not like that now. Or maybe it never was like this, it was just easier to get away with it because we didn't have a fully-transparent, 24-7 digital world.

From my vantage point, a ton of energy is wasted in trying to convince others of our "rightness", even when we have facts on our side. But here's the problem: other people believe just as strongly in *their* rightness and *their* set of facts which support their position. We are in an endless tug-of-war where no one wins the war and we are all tuckered out from the battle with no victors.

Whether it's at work or around the dining room table over the holidays, consider adopting the Two Rights position instead. You are right. And they are too. You both feel strongly about your positions, and both of you are worthy of respect. One way to bridge that gap is to initiate the strategy of The Middle Way. Step up to try to understand their perspective, the context by which they came to that conclusion, and the personal histories that may be influencing their beliefs. Suspend your desire for rightness in favor of empathy and understanding.

Ask questions. Be curious.

Instead of making even more statements trying to make your points *finally* understood, consider asking more probing questions. Why do you think that way? On what aspects of the topic do we have agreement? What can we do to find a respectful middle ground that allows both of us to preserve our "rightness" without eroding our relationship? How can we be more mindful of each other's feelings?

I grew up in a household with winners and losers. In any conflict, someone ended up on top and the other caved. It is this fixed mindset that gets us into trouble. We work so hard to try to win an argument that we forget what the end goal is: *peace*.

A regular meditation practice will help you regularly execute The Middle Way with those people for whom you have negative feelings. An especially powerful tool is performing the Loving Kindness, or Metta, Meditation.

It is a simple practice that involves getting grounded and centered, repeating the statements "May I be happy. May I be well. May I be safe. May I be peaceful and free from suffering." And truly feel what it feels like to have those characteristics. Then, move on to imagine those same ideals for those you dearly love, "May you be happy. May you be well. May you be safe. May you be peaceful and free from suffering." And sink into the feeling of having that be a reality for those closest to you. After a few moments, expand the visualization to include every single living being on the planet: "May all beings be happy. May they all be well. May they be safe. May they be peaceful and free from suffering." And imagine that lofty, beautiful vision. Let your heart feel it. By doing so, you are consciously expanding your ability to empathize and show compassion, both of which are key attributes to successful leadership and collaboration.

Over time, you will find that you are able to be present with others who are in direct opposition to you, show empathy toward them, and soften your angry or annoyed edges.

GUERILLA POSITIVITY

What messages have you surrounded yourself with beyond the words that come out of your mouth or through your fingers? We get to choose every day the messages that are in our field of vision, and we get to choose how we share those messages with others.

I'm a big believer in guerrilla positivity, blasting the world with goodness at every turn. Here are but a few examples of how I add empowering messaging in everyday ways:

- My home wi-fi has been named "LifeIsGood" instead of the default gobbledeegook the cable provider assigns.

- The bumper sticker on my car says, "What are you grateful for?" which puts a smile on the faces of everyone driving behind me.

- The workout shirts I wear always have an empowering statement such as "The force is strong with this one," or "Life is tough, but so am I".

- My coffee cups say, "Dreams don't have to be realistic," and "Be bad@ss every day".

- My laptop password is a phrase that reminds me of the most important thing in the world to me.

In fact, I have gone so far as to take guerrilla positivity to the streets. I have several small "You are beautiful" stickers in my purse at all times just in case an opportunity presents itself. Sometimes I will leave one with a server who did an especially great job. Other times I'll give it to a child who does something nice for another. I've been known on more than one occasion to stick one on a ladies' restroom mirror. (Shhh … don't tell anyone!)

Keep an eye out for ways you can perform guerrilla positivity. How can you brighten your day with uplifting messaging while empowering another? It doesn't take a lot of effort, and the trail of goodness you leave in your wake will be noticeable.

SUPERSTRATEGY:
TWO WORDS

We've all had diarrhea of the mouth at one time or another. Using words, words, and more words to try to convey our point to another. Sometimes, as if there is an inverse relationship of words-to-impact, the more we talk, the less we actually get accomplished or reach our desired outcome. Regardless if it's at work or in our personal lives, oftentimes less is more when it comes to sending the perfect message.

When you find yourself running off at the mouth while in a challenging dialogue with someone, consider hitting the pause button.

Take a moment to find the two perfect words that will elevate the energy of the exchange.

In fact, even if it's not a difficult situation and you just want to more deeply connect with someone—your team members, your prospects and customers, your loved ones, your neighbors, or the stranger you just met in line—find the most efficient way to say something powerful and inspiring. Two words—when spoken with sincerity—can be exactly what people need to hear to brighten their day, make them feel special, appreciated and supported, and solidify your bond. Here are a few to consider:

- I apologize.

- Love you.

- Tell me.

- What's up?

- Great job!

- Next time.

- Nice haircut!

- Forgive me.

- Please help.

- Stay strong.

- I'm here.

- Rock on.

Messages are the bridges from one person to another. Our minds and hearts get connected (or disconnected) based on how thoughtful we are with our communications. By taking a mindful moment to carefully choose the words we use—verbally and in writing—we will dramatically improve our relationships, our performance, our earning power, and our impact in our communities.

SELF-REFLECTION:
MESSAGES

What are your strengths in this focus area?

_____

_____

_____

_____

What are your opportunities for growth?

_____

_____

_____

_____

What specific life experiences came up for you as you read through this chapter? What was the impact to you personally and professionally?

_____

_____

_____

_____

How would improving your activity and awareness in this focus area help you reach your goals?

_____

_____

_____

_____

What are the strategies that resonated with you the most?

- **Polarity Potholes**

- **I Over You**

- **Yes, and**

- **Delightful Networking**

- **Thought-full Emails**

- **Spewer vs. Doer**

- **The Middle Way**

- **Guerilla Positivity**

- **Two Words (SuperStrategy)**

What is one action you will take to increase your performance in this area, and by when will you do it?

_____

_____

_____

_____

CHAPTER 9

MEDIA

....

In case you haven't noticed, we've entered a new era, an era where technology has become more than a tool to help make life easier. It is now fully woven into the fabric of our existence. Wake up? Look at your device. Go to the bathroom? Look at your device. Eat a meal by yourself? Look at your device. Waiting for the light to turn green? Quickly look at your device. Sitting in a boring meeting? Surreptitiously look at your device. Participate on a conference call or webinar? Deep-dive into your device. Standing in line at the airport, DMV, or grocery store? Look at your device. Relaxing at the end of a long day of work? Look at your bigger-screen device. Drifting off to sleep? Look at your devi … zzz. We are waaaay too connected to our machines, and it is having an impact on our health.

Do yourself a favor and replace some of the time you are spending on the glowing rectangle with good old-fashioned brain-time. When everyone else is whipping out their phones, opt instead to simply sit in silence for a few minutes to reset your mental state and become present. Your performance will improve.

I grew up with four television channels. The biggest technological advance in our household was that our tiny television was in color. I still had to get up to turn the knob from channel 2 where I was watching "Zoom!" on PBS to channel 13 where the latest repeat of "Gilligan's Island" or "I Love Lucy" was playing. (Lucille Ball was a comedy genius, and I knew back then that I wanted to perform comedy for a living.) My friends and I would watch cartoons and comedies after school, sing during the commercials, and goof around during the slow parts. The local park and swimming pool were favorite hangouts in the summertime. Life was, for lack of a better word, unplugged.

If your childhood was pre-Internet, things were pretty simple back then. If you wanted something, you needed to walk or bike to the store for it. If you wanted to talk with someone, you needed a telephone (my favorite was my pink Princess rotary). Movies were delivered one of two ways: either you went to the movie theatre or you watched TV Movies of the Week. In school, we communicated with paper!

Children in my daughter's generation—Digital Natives—have grown up with devices. While they have literally everything they need (and certainly much of what they don't) at the touch of a finger, many of them have missed out on those precious unplugged experiences. When my daughter says she had a "conversation" with someone, nine times out of ten they didn't even *talk*—they texted. Here's the thing about texting—it's a non-localized asynchronous communication model, meaning body and facial language, tone, and most importantly, *energy* are not present in the relationships my daughter and her generation are developing. They are bereft of the kaleidoscope of inputs that help them sort out the true messages people are sending. They can also very easily "ghost", which means you walk away without having to actually walk away. You simply stop responding and check out.

Now, add to the mix unlimited distractions, eye candy, visual anesthetization, critical civic and global information, compelling art, and anything else that would make Bacchus back away. Technology use and abuse don't just apply to "those damned Millennials" anymore. *Everyone* has fallen into the digital abyss. There is now such a condition as "text neck" that chiropractors are treating, which is a reverse curvature of the cervical spine because of our constant hunching over our screens. People are struggling to keep up with their jobs, feeling overwhelmed with the sheer enormity of the inputs coming at them, and feel robbed of precious time just to care for themselves and possibly even have some fun. For many of us, time is the most precious resource. We simply don't have enough of it to truly enjoy our lives. But we do have time to read that next email. Or read an article or two on a news site. Or scan through our social media feeds for "a few minutes". Or click on that video clip. And another. And another. Before we know it, the day has "gotten away" from us.

Yes, the day has gotten away from you. And me. And the entire modern world. One innocent click at a time.

Pac-man was one of the first video games I remember playing. I loved going with my friends to the arcade. While Space Invaders, Asteroids, and Donkey Kong devoured my quarters, Pac-man was my absolute favorite. A cute little yellow man-circle (Us) chomp-chomp-chomped his way through the maze (Life) by eating all of the small dots (time) to get to the center (our goal) without getting destroyed by the ghosts (our enemies) before time runs out (our death). The saddest moment playing Pac-man or any of these games was seeing those two ominous words: GAME OVER.

Let's bring the Pac-man analogy into our current landscape of mindful performance. Imagine every time we boot up our computers or turn on our devices, we are playing Pac-man. But it's real this time. And every bit of content—regardless of its impor-tance or easy-to-justify relevance—is a dot, but we just keep eating eating eating dots instead of moving to the middle to get to our goal.

That is our relationship to digital content.

We are Pac-manning our lives away, click by click.

AT HOME

....

We can establish healthier habits and stronger boundaries with our digital delights in order to create more time for our own pursuits instead of losing ourselves in our screens.

TECHNOLOGY MEDICINE

It's hard to argue with the fact that spending too much time on media is draining us of our life force energy and certainly contributing to a lack of motivation. However, there are certain kinds of media that can help our performance *if* we wisely choose the mediums and the time durations.

How can media actually motivate us to take strategic action toward our goal? It's all about choosing the outlets that have the most amount of empowerment and the least amount of marketing manipulation. There are scads of helpful productivity tools you can use to better your life. For example, I struggled for many years with my weight and had an adversarial relationship with food. I gave what I put in my mouth far too much emotional power, often turning a blind eye to what food actually is designed to be: *fuel*. Several years ago, I started using an app that logged every single thing I ate and drank over a period of several months. By diligently recording what I was taking into my body, I found a new level of awareness of my relationship to food and permanently shed more than fifty pounds. (YAY!) It made what was once a purely emotional process into one that I could track with numbers. Contrary to what humans will do, numbers don't lie, manipulate me into a false sense of deserving, or hide my transgressions with naughty carbs. It told me the *truth*. And that truth—when I eat X amount of calories every day, I lost weight—was what set me free from the treacherous binds of emotional eating.

You can use the same concept to find media sites and apps that actually support you. You can use media to your advantage to motivate you to take that all-important mindful next step in the creation of your dreams. For example, use

- a meditation app like those we discussed in Chapter 4,

- a fitness app that helps you track your movement practice,

- an electronic log that records the number of smoke-free days, or

- a motivational video you can watch every morning that centers you and gets you focused on consciously creating your day.

Opt to play calming music that lowers your levels of cortisol and increases your sense of balance and contentment instead of having the television on so you can listen to all the latest bad news. Mindlab International conducted a study that measured anxiety levels based on music played. A song called *Weightless* by Marconi Union was identified as the most relaxing song to participants, resulting in a staggering 65% reduction in anxiety.[12] Thanks to the collective contributions of researchers, neuroscientists, and sound healing experts, its lulling tones included all the aspects our brains want in order to bring us into a deeper state of relaxation. (Don't drive to it!) I use this song as my alarm, gently bridging me from sleep state to alertness. It's a lot more pleasant to get a jump-start on the day when I feel the warm blanket of beautiful music surround me.

CONSCIOUS BINGEING

A few years back, television programming was a wasteland of reality shows and wacky competition programs. It was easy to forego watching too much TV because nearly everything on the boob tube was crap. Now we have an endless choice of incredibly well-written shows that are expertly produced and feature our favorite actors. They have compelling storylines, heart-wrenching drama, and gut-busting humor. You can lose yourself in another world for hours and hours on end with one simple click.

Our culture has romanticized the binge-watch. It seems that nearly everyone has a show (or ten) that they are currently devouring at every spare moment. Entire weekends are dedicated to digesting complete seasons of new shows, with fans proclaiming on social media how wonderful their extended viewing experience was. I too have caught myself bingeing on more than one occasion, the most recent being an obsessive nonstop consumption of HBO's "Veep" during a week when I was recovering from a surgical procedure. While I loved the show and highly recommend it, I don't recommend watching six seasons over five days.

As someone who is always seeking out a mindful approach to daily living, I observe my mood when I binge on media. While I am watching must-see TV, I am definitely enjoying a hedonistic "I deserve this!" sense of pleasure similar to what a delicious meal, delectable chocolate, or let's be honest, great sex will give you. There is definitely a rush of endorphins when we experience great art and beauty in all its forms. However, bingeing also brings with it a numbness that makes us forget about the passing of time. It is the slow morphine drip that quiets the frantic mind and soothes the weary heart. When we binge, we essentially give up that time that could be spent living our own lives in favor of observing fictional characters experiencing theirs. I fear that as artificial intelligence becomes more popular, we will resemble the corpulent people from "WALL-E" flying around on our Barcaloungers, drinking sugar, and having screens in front of us at all times.

We are losing ourselves to the binge.

What makes managing our media consumption even more difficult is that it is not unlike a drug. Kicking the binge-watching habit is tantamount to treating an addiction. You may go through withdrawal. You may get agitated and restless. You may try to rationalize that you'll watch "only one more season". You may convince yourself that bingeing is a form of relaxation and you don't see anything wrong with it; after all, *everybody* is doing it. This is the trap. It lulls us into thinking that numbing out is the same thing as relaxing; it's *not*. Instead, it is keeping us on the serotonin drip one episode at a time while our lives continue on without us.

The media binge is not limited to watching programs on subscription channels such as Netflix, Hulu, Amazon, and the dozens of others. It can also be playing video games. Or it can be spending an entire evening on Facebook or Pinterest. Or watching sports and other competition shows. How many times have you or someone close to you spent hours and hours in front of a screen?

I grew up in a household where most of the weekends were about sports: we watched college football all day Saturday and the NFL all day Sunday. We not only watched the pre-game and post-game coverage, but we also watched both (or sometimes three) games that lasted several hours each, all while chowing down on nachos and other assorted game snacks. When I got older, those games were accompanied by adult beverages galore. This behavior of giving up my life to television was certainly a contributing factor to my lifelong struggle with weight and depression.

If you are a binge-watcher, please know that I am not trying to shame you in any way. Rather, it is to bring to your awareness the potential price you are paying for that habit. When you are watching media or playing games for hours on end, you are *not* moving your body. You are *not* taking purposeful action toward your health and abundance. You are *not* engaging in meaningful dialogue with those important to you. You are *not* feeding your brain with inspiration, education, and empowerment. The goal here is not to make you feel badly about the choices you have made in the past. Trust me, I am not someone to preach about TV watching. In college I was selected to be on MTV's first game show, "Remote Control", precisely because of my vast knowledge of useless facts pertaining to television. However, I am encouraging you to ...

be mindful with your media consumption.

Go into your marathon sessions with eyes wide open, seeing the cost-benefit analysis for what it is. You *do* pay a price for checking out, and I am inviting you to be a part of the negotiation process. Ask yourself what price you are willing to pay to numb out. Are there places where you can put some boundaries or limits on your consumption, just as you would if you were to attend a party and limit the number of appetizers, drinks, or desserts you consume?

If you find yourself in a depressed state, look to the amount of media you are taking in. Chances are, screen time is one of the factors that is creating that state of malaise. No matter what, make good, mindful choices when you binge. Choose only the best of the best. Make it worth the price.

BOOK SCANNING

There is something very rewarding about reading an entire book (you're almost there!). It is one of those rare experiences that requires time, patience, and desire. Reading that last sentence of the last page, closing the book, rubbing the cover, and putting it on your bookshelf is immensely satisfying. We feel smarter, better, and richer for having done it. We also know that reading is a habit of highly-successful people, and we know we *should* read more books. But most of us don't. Why? Because they take so much gosh-darned time—time we simply don't have.

Instead of foregoing book reading altogether, let's look at a viable alternative: Book scanning. Authors understand the time challenges of the modern reader, and many of them are adjusting their writing and formatting styles accordingly. More often than not, nonfiction books are being written for scan-ability.

If there is a book you'd like to read, pick it up at the library or book-store and read through the Table of Contents to see what the highlights are. Make note of the chapters that are of most impor-tance to you. You may want to dive a little deeper into those. Then, just flip through the book, one page at a time, scanning for the most important aspects of the teaching. They will be the headers, underlined, bolded, or highlighted text, or graphics. Read those over a time or two and let your eyes wander down to pick up any extra bits of wisdom. You'll be amazed how much information and inspiration you will receive over an hour of scanning a good book. Take those nuggets of awesome and take one tangible action to act upon. When you do so, you'll have certainly seen a return on investment.

Literary purists may balk at this mindful performance strategy, saying it is disrespectful to the author and/or the material. They will argue that the author wrote the material to be consumed as a whole. As a multiple award-winning author, I would counter that assertion; authors want readers to engage with our material (to whatever degree they wish) in the hopes that it will make a positive impact on their lives (if only for a moment). It is far better for you to consume a book in scannable chunks than to not pick it up at all.

Go ahead. Get that book you've been dying to read but didn't have the time. There's always time—maybe that's what you can read while waiting in line! And, of course, if you leave the TV off and don't spend hours on Facebook or YouTube, you'll have more time to read a book.

AT WORK

....

Just because we are at work doesn't mean we are exempt from the performance-sapping damage our digital devices can wield. Here are some things to consider in order to maximize your interactions with your screens during the workday.

SANCTIONED DISTRACTIONS

It's easy to let media distractions rob us of our work productivity as well. While many organizations now have filters in place to keep people away from social media and video sites, it doesn't keep us from sneaking peeks on our phones when the work grind gets to be too much. Even if we discount the furtive glances on our phones, there are many other distractions lurking throughout the seemingly innocent workday.

Do you find yourself spending an inordinate amount of time endlessly researching when you could have stopped hours ago? Do you watch videos or read blogs of industry experts just to keep yourself away from the wretched pile of *actual* work that awaits you? Are you dabbling with new technology solutions instead of getting what author Cal Newport called "Deep Work" done?

If you are an entrepreneur, your challenges are even greater. How easy is it to waste massive chunks of time poking around on LinkedIn and Facebook to "build your online presence", "connect with your customers," or "do competitive analysis"? Salespeople are also tempted to lollygag on sanctioned media sites because it keeps them one step away from directly connecting with their prospects and customers, which may include the word they never want to hear: "no." It's really easy to look busy on the computer. It's quite another to actually be productive. As sales professionals, we don't get paid for how we *appear* to be doing business; we get paid when we actually *close* business.

Don't let the allure of the sanctioned distraction keep you from reaching your goal.

As with any mindful practice, the best solution is to intentionally carve out a chunk of time when you will be on social media. I recommend that you do it *after* you have accomplished the one, two, or three strategically-relevant tasks you absolutely, positively *will* do in support of your goals. Don't jump on social sites right away in the morning because it is far too easy to chomp-chomp-chomp your time away. Before you know it, it's mid-morning and you haven't even gotten into the meat of your workday. Give yourself permission to take in media during prescribed times, and then don't do anything other than actual work or intentional rest during the other times. You will quickly find that not only will your performance and profits skyrocket, your mood will also naturally elevate by rejecting the noise that distracts you from your objectives.

MONEY-MAKING MEDIA

After reading all of these cautionary tales about media consumption, you may be thinking that I am either a luddite or a techno-hater. Nothing could be further from the truth! I *love* technology and media, especially when it is in support of my professional goals. In order to be a successful salesperson and leader, purposeful use of media can actually *make* you money.

Chances are that an aspect of your job is to connect with others in an attempt to persuade them to buy a product, service, or concept.

Every single one of us is in sales.

We are all trying to sell an idea or a solution to someone, whether it is to our customers, our colleagues, our superiors, or our families. Using media can help get you there.

The adage of "A picture is worth a thousand words" is true. Using pictures—and better yet, video—will go a long way toward connecting with your buyers on an emotional level, the level that actually parts them with their money. People want to think they buy logically, but that just isn't true. They may pre-qualify with logic, but they *buy* emotionally. And emotions are far easier to stir with video than with words alone.

My business skyrocketed when I started to use video email to follow up with prospective clients for speaking engagements.

It wasn't enough to send an email containing flowery words that described my energy, expertise, and passion; sending them a video *showing* me embodying those characteristics was the key. Our buyers are impacted by the onslaught of media just like us, and most are no longer reading–they are scanning. (Thank you, by the way, for reading my book! Yay you! You are keeping your brain strong!) In addition to scanning, they are also *watching*.

Make your content watchable.

Use the tricks of the media trade to get them to pay attention.

Posting updates on social media can sell your products and services. No matter how great your last LinkedIn post or article was (I recommend writing posts versus articles; they are viewed far more frequently because people perceive themselves as not having the time to commit to reading an entire article), you will be lost in the vortex of the unviewable if you don't include an emotionally compelling photo. When you are reaching out to your buyers either individually or through your social network or website, ask yourself, in what way can I use media to make a relatable connection with their hearts and a logical connection with their minds? Both are needed for them to commit.

You can also use video or live streaming to show your tribe the kind of warm, funny, relatable person you are. Remember, people buy from people they like. Use media to highlight your likability. Technology has advanced to such a degree that you can literally have all of the tools you need to run your own content creation agency, all within your smartphone. The solutions are there; use them to make more money.

FLYING FREE

One of the keys to giving your brain some down time is to find empty spaces of time when you opt to *be* instead of *do*. In my humble opinion, one of the best opportunities is during air travel.

I used to love to work on airplanes. They were reasonably quiet (especially with my standard-issue earbuds), free from distraction, and allowed a big chunk of time when I couldn't be anywhere else. I loved the feeling of hitting 10,000 feet when I could rush to get my laptop out to catch up on email, write a blog post or two, or chip away on my latest book or presentation. However, as air travel has become more uncomfortable and people have become less civil, it became less pleasant to work in the sky. I'm a petite five-foot-three (on a good day!) and can barely find a comfortable position in which to work. With the tray table jutting into my gut because the #%&^ passenger in front of me reclines his chair, coupled with my neighbor manspreading into my space, it is just too much hassle for less and less payoff. (Of course, first class makes it comfier, but there is still great benefit to unplugging for an extended period of time.)

Even if you don't work on an airplane, you may be tempted to pony up the dough for Wi-Fi, so you can continue to text, email, and surf to your heart's content. You may be anxious to catch up on the latest episode of your favorite show or watch that action flick that will make time quickly pass. I get it. It's tempting to use the flight as down-time. However, by doing so, you are still plugged into the Matrix, not using that juicy time to either amp up for the trip ahead or rewind from the hard work that is behind you.

Consider taking your next travel for business sans screens. Crack open a good book—maybe even one that has nothing to do with work or professional development! Can you imagine? WOW! Or you can listen to a podcast that will inspire you to take specific actions that will assist you on your journey to greater profitability and purpose. Or, if you are totally wild and crazy, you can just sit. Observe your surroundings. Breathe into your body. Do your own creative visualization on how you want the rest of your day to unfold. The possibilities are endless. It's a great time to practice mindfulness while establishing a healthier relationship with media.

ALL DAY

....

Taking a proactive role in consciously managing your relationship with media no matter where you are will help energize you and keep your eyes on what's truly important: the realization of your vision.

BY THE NUMBERS

Like it or not, we largely measure progress, competency, and success by numbers. As I shared before, numbers don't lie (even when we try to convince ourselves that the rising number on the scale "can't possibly be right"). Numbers certainly don't tell the whole story, but they do provide a standard, nonvariable metric by which we can measure where we are now compared to a goal. When we look at our numbers, be it monthly sales quotas, new recruits for a multi-level marketing organization, consecutive days of exercise, or word count for that latest book, they give us a framework of understanding as to our current status in relation to an objective. Your use of social media can be treated in the same manner in order to assess the degree to which media and screen time impact your performance.

When we read statistics that say we spend at least half our days looking at screens, we often think to ourselves, "Yeah, that's for most people, but I'm not *that* bad." How do you know that? Do you know *for sure*? Are you assuming your usage is so much lower than others, or do you have numbers to back up your claim?

Instead of merely assuming your usage numbers are lower than average, take a moment to actually measure it. Install an app that will track how much time your phone has been active, how many sites you have visited, and how often you clicked. Then, and only then, will you have an accurate picture of your relationship to the digital world. Examine your numbers over an extended period of time, preferably at least a month, and record the results. At the end of the month, take an unflinching look at the data and decide for yourself where you stand with your usage and if you are comfortable with it. If it is higher than you would like, start taking precautionary measures such as removing apps you know are certified time-wasters (games, shopping, news sites) and burying nonessential apps (I'm talkin' to *you*, Facebook) so you'll have to make a conscious decision to hunt for them when you want to use them. Changing your screen colors to grayscale can help reduce your desire to click. You may even consider putting a sticky note on your phone saying, "Is it necessary?" to remind you to limit your screen time. By implementing these small but consistent acts, you'll find you will gradually decrease your time spent hunched over the glow.

Another number to consider as you monitor your media usage is to go through your Netflix and Hulu queues (or whatever content-delivery networks you utilize) and identify the shows you watch every week. Look at the timestamp on each video and list them on a spreadsheet. Add them up and see how much time you are giving away to entertainment. Two hours? Five hours? Ten? Twenty-five? Think about how many minutes you would gain each week if you removed just one show from your queue! Consider what you would actually get accomplished if you used that time performing highly-focused action items pertaining to your right livelihood, reading an engaging book that contributes to your personal and professional development, or simply caring for yourself with movement, meditation, healthy meal preparation, time in nature, or even sleep.

By taking the time to crunch the numbers, you will be armed with the information you need to make informed, conscious decisions about your media usage. You will no longer be passively siphoning time away from yourself, instead opting to create more chunks of time that will actually serve you.

Numbers are your friend. Don't be afraid of them.

They can help you create a more mindful relationship with your devices.

SOLO AND SMARTPHONE-FREE

One way to free yourself from the clutches of the media monster is to create new habits that allow you to practice presence and mindfulness. Before you get all defensive or start to justify why your media usage isn't something to worry about, I invite you to consider when was the last time you did the following solitary activities, device-free:

- Eat a meal

- Stand in line

- Sit in a waiting area (airport, bus station, doctor's office, office lobby)

- Go to the bathroom

- Lie in bed

- Attend a function (networking, meeting, wedding)

Did you automatically reach for your smartphone when given just a few minutes of quiet time to do nothing? If so, cut yourself some slack. Nearly everyone does it. (Me too.) However, that doesn't mean it needs to remain that way. It's just a habit, and habits can be broken by taking intentional, consistent action.

Instead of being vague about your media use, try setting some small but specific goals that will set you up for success. Below are some helpful scenarios where you can become more aware of your thoughts, sensations, and surroundings instead of reaching for the smartphone.

- **Upon waking, don't turn on your phone right away.** If you need it for your alarm, only use it for that purpose. Lie there in silence for a few minutes before you embark upon your day. Let your transition from the sleep state to consciousness be a gentle one with positive visualizations instead of the latest noise floating around the World Wide Web.

- **Go to the bathroom by yourself.** Leave the phone on the bedside stand. Not only is it more hygienic, it is also allowing you to actually notice what is around you ("I never noticed how many tiles there are on the wall! Have those dust buffalos in the corner always been there? A new towel would be perfect for that towel rack.").

- **Brush your teeth with purpose.** Notice how the bristles feel against your teeth and gums. Feel the toothpaste foaming as you brush. Do you always brush with the same hand? Try switching it up and notice how that feels. Was it awkward? Did that make you feel slightly agitated? How does the water feel when it sloshes around your mouth? Paying attention to sensations allows you to strengthen your ability to focus, which bleeds into the rest of your day.

- **Don't check out before you check out.** When you are waiting in line—at the grocery store, coffee shop, doctor's office, anywhere that has you standing in queue—resist the temptation to check email, send a text, read the news, or catch up on social media. Simply stand and notice what is going on around you without judging it. How are people treating each other? Are they looking each other in the eyes? What noises are going on around you? How would you characterize the comfort level of the environment? How does your body feel standing there? Are you in need of some progressive muscle relaxation in order to release tension and stress?

- **Start peppering your day with screen-free moments.** A few mindful minutes here and there will add up, creating a greater sense of awareness of your surroundings, your physical body, and your emotional states. The more aware you become, the better you will be able to genuinely listen to those around you—whether it's your team members, your customers, your loved ones, or strangers you encounter during the course of your day.

SUPERSTRATEGY:
MEDIA FASTS

I'm a big fan of the fast. Whether it's a nutritional cleanse or a digital one, there is value to resetting the system by bringing it to zero. The fasting process not only hot-cuts your addictions (try cutting out sugar, caffeine, alcohol, and processed foods for a week and see how much you miss them!) but it also gives helpful insights into the emotional undercurrents that run through our habituated actions.

There is an art to accomplishing a fast. One must be acutely aware of one's actions at all times, ensuring that unconscious behaviors don't occur. Emotional and physical preparations are a must. Strengthen your will by incorporating additional movement, reading, and accountability. Acknowledge that fasting is inherently challenging, but you are stronger than electronic addiction. Here are a few media fasts you may want to incorporate into your life:

- **Daily**—Make one hour every day completely device-free/electronics-free (preferably at the end of the evening so you get a good night's rest). Put it in your calendar and set an alarm to remind you of the cutoff. Give yourself a ten-minute warning to wrap up any conversations or threads.

- **Weekly**—Take one weekend day and keep your phone in the bedroom. If you go out of the house with someone else who has a phone (who doesn't nowadays?), leave yours at home. Challenge yourself to get through the entire day without so much as a click until you set your alarm for bed. If you do, give yourself a healthy reward for tackling a major undertaking!

- **Monthly**—See if you can carve out a hundred hours of non-electronics time by the end of the month. Tally up the minutes you spend enjoying nature, reading, moving or sitting still every single day, and if you hit the 100 milestone, celebrate your victory with something special. You deserve it. It's an incredible accomplishment.

- **Quarterly/Yearly**—Take a multi-day media blackout to powerfully reset your relationship with media. Take a vacation to a location that has little reception. Lock your phone in the hotel safe. Climb a mountaintop if you have to. Create a big chunk of screen-free time to put yourself in the thick of your awareness. Make sure you have other fun or challenging activities to keep you occupied as your mind starts to crave the outside world.

By purposefully reorienting your relationship to media, you will become acutely aware of the impact screen time has had on your psyche and how much time you will gain back by cutting the cord, even if it's just for a few extra moments every day. By consistently and mindfully addressing this major aspect of modern living, you will move into the driver's seat of your own success and be empowered to make better choices both online and off.

SELF-REFLECTION: MEDIA

What are your strengths in this focus area?

_____

_____

_____

_____

What are your opportunities for growth?

_____

_____

_____

_____

What specific life experiences came up for you as you read through this chapter? What was the impact to you personally and professionally?

_____

_____

_____

_____

How would improving your activity and awareness in this focus area help you reach your goals?

_____

_____

_____

_____

What are the strategies that resonated with you the most?

- **Technology Medicine**

- **Conscious Bingeing**

- **Book Scanning**

- **Sanctioned Distractions**

- **Money-making Media**

- **Flying Free**

- **By the Numbers**

- **Solo and Smartphone-free**

- **Media Fasts (SuperStrategy)**

What is one action you will take to increase your performance in this area, and by when will you do it?

_____

_____

_____

_____

CHAPTER 10

MESSES

....

I grew up with a neatnik. My mother was a Grade A "wiper", never missing an opportunity to use a sponge to spruce up the counter-tops in our cozy apartment kitchen. Living in small apartments for much of my life afforded me the opportunity to establish a healthy relationship with objects and the space that contains them.

It turns out those early teachings about everything having its place and cleaning up after myself served me well both personally and professionally. After shifting my career from management in corporate America to diving into the pool of holistic healing, I began to expand my knowledge and education on the power of space.

I dabbled in the art and practice of Feng Shui, an ancient Chinese system of object placement and orientation that is said to affect the movement of energy in any given space. Personally, I could tell the difference in not only how I felt physically and emotionally but also my performance when I was more mindful of where and how I placed my objects. Have you ever entered a space and just felt comfortable because of its breathability and flow? Conversely, have you ever felt ill at ease in some spaces and you didn't know why?

Our spaces are reflections of us.

When we lose control of our physical space because of clutter or uncleanliness, that same lack of control bleeds into other areas of our world. Being mindful of our space doesn't mean we need to have an immaculate, perfectly Feng-Shuied house that Martha Stewart would envy. It's simply about paying attention to your environment and the objects surrounding you at home, at work, and on the road. Do you feel calm, cared for, and empowered when you are there, or do you have a quiet level of discomfort and anxiousness? Are the objects surrounding you *supporting* you or sabotaging you?

Many people I have counseled over the years have had an unhealthy, disempowered relationship with their physical environments. Taking command of our space is tough, and it can trigger

- a lot of feelings of obligation ("I can't throw that away!"),

- fear ("What if I need it and it's not there?"), and

- even abandonment ("That's important to me!")

It's *our* stuff! We are like Linus and his beloved blanket. While it may provide some degree of comfort to be surrounded by our possessions (after all, we worked hard to get them!), it ultimately harms us if the maintenance, upkeep, and recycling requires more energy than we are willing or able to commit to. Meanwhile, we are sucking our thumbs with our eyes closed, holding on for dear life to our stuff.

We can, however, mindfully manage our messes. Since it requires a strong will to make tough decisions, we may need some extra help along the way. Do not hesitate to call in for backup If you are one of those people who would benefit from receiving mental and emotional support by a counselor or organizational support from a dear friend or a professional organizer. This, like any major undertaking, may be better addressed with a team versus alone.

There is no shame in getting the help we need. *Ever.*

Consider checking out the National Association of Professional Organizers as an initial resource if you want help in rebooting your space.

Time, money, energy, and space are interconnected; what happens to one affects the others. When you have more time, you can positively impact your money, energy levels, and space. You may be thinking, "So what if I'm disorganized? I am making great money, so I don't really care about how messy my space is." You may, in fact, be making sufficient or even extraordinary income, but there are other areas in your life that may be suffering if you are not in harmony with your physical surroundings.

The more organized you are, the faster you accomplish your tasks or get from point A to point B. There is a monetary and emotional value to your time. In addition, any time you waste digging through piles and rifling in drawers could have been spent on your personal health and wellness. You could have taken that extra ten minutes it took to find the elusive file to take a brisk walk outside or even close your eyes and sit still for a few moments to reset and practice your mindfulness.

When you are in right relation with your physical world, you will make more time for yourself. You will get more done because you won't be wasting precious minutes sifting through distractions. You will earn more money because you will be maximizing your effort with the right tools. You will have more fun because you will be supported by the positive flow of object-energy around you instead of being suffocated by it.

Go ahead. Clean up. You deserve it.

AT HOME

Your environment reflects you, so you want it to be as efficient and pleasant as possible. Here are a few mess-management strategies you can use to keep the energy of your home flowing fully and freely.

PURPOSEFUL PLACES

A few years back I was in desperate need of help in dealing with a growing paper explosion in my home office. Piles of statements, reports, invoices, contracts, and periodicals were a constant presence that quietly mocked me, telling me I was failing on the job of managing my household and key aspects of my business. It got so bad that I felt like the paper monster was going to crush me. I reached out to my dear friend Elizabeth, a fellow speaker and professional organizer. Elizabeth spent the day with me to uncover all the nasties lurking in the piles. She helped me figure out how to process each piece of paper and set me up with a few amazing, simple systems I could consistently and successfully use to take back control of the paper and other aspects of household management. (I made the label maker and colored file folders my friends.) The result was a far more productive work environment that allowed me to focus on important activities which very quickly netted me more income.

Where does your incoming mail (bills, statements, offers, and other scraps of important paper) go once it arrives in your mailbox? Is it a pile that expands and grows, or do you have an organizer that allows you to easily tuck it away without irritating you? Everything needs a resting place, ideally one that is intuitive, practical, easy to access, and pleasing to the eye. I have organizers for my cords, office supplies, computer peripherals, and anything else that seems to spread out over time. Look around and see what you can do to rein in your messes. Invest in your infrastructure, and it will support you in your endeavors.

FIX-IT LIST

Is there anything broken or missing in your home? A burned-out light bulb from the bathroom mirror? A cabinet door that doesn't close properly? A fixer-upper project you have been meaning to get to but haven't found the time? Okay. No worries. Get up *right now* and fix it if you can. If you need someone's assistance, take out a post-it note and write down the item that needs repair. Put the note somewhere where you will act on it either later today or early tomorrow. Go ahead. Do it. I'll wait.

If our external environment reflects our internal environment, then let's make sure no part of us is broken or missing. **Our goal is to be whole and complete beings, working as designed.** Addressing the items on our Fix-it List helps us move to that whole and complete state.

Thinking about it doesn't count; we must act.

If the fixer-upper project is major, don't get discouraged. Just take the very first step required to fix it. Remember the Who's Going to do What by When strategy. Call a repair professional by tomorrow. Once you execute that task, the next step will present itself: schedule time to have it repaired. So many of us get caught in the trap of thinking about the enormity of a project that we check out because we get overwhelmed. Instead, consider taking that one *and only* first step. "Put one foot in front of the other, and soon you'll be walking 'cross the floor!"

Even spending a few minutes cleaning out a junk drawer or going through your closet to purge items you no longer love will help boost your performance. You'll spend less time searching for what you are looking for and more on creating!

HOME SPA RETREAT

Ahhh … the spa. It is a sanctuary of peace and restoration that women and men alike use to rest, relax, and rejuvenate. There is nothing quite like the zen-like energy of a high-quality spa. It is a retreat for the soul.

Most of us can't afford the time or money to regularly visit these bastions of bliss. But that shouldn't stop us from creating a facsimile of the spa retreat.

Our senses impact our mood, so choose wisely when creating your personal sanctuary.

Let's see how we can recreate it in our own homes. First, your personal spa retreat should be free from disruptive noise. When you are at a spa, you don't hear blaring televisions or raised voices. (If you do, you are in the wrong spa.) Instead, you hear gentle music that lulls you to a deeper state of relaxation. Reduce the volume in your home, opting for music over television. Avoid yelling from one room to another. Do your best to make it pleasant to the ears.

Second, create a comfortable space where you can intentionally relax. Just as a spa has lovely-but-sparse décor, your home spa retreat can have the same characteristics. Even if it's just your favorite easy chair, have a cozy blanket with tea nearby so you can cuddle up with a book. Remove any old magazines or junk crowding you. Let your restoration space be one that breathes.

Finally, make your retreat smell good. When you walk into a spa, one of the first things you'll notice is how delightful is smells. There is usually subtle aromatherapy wafting through the air. You can do the same. Get an aromatherapy diffuser and use it throughout the day. Use citrus after a pungent meal to refresh the space. Use eucalyptus to keep you energized. Use florals to calm you at the end of the day.

AT WORK

There are 24 hours in a day, eight of which should be spent sleeping. (We'll be learning more on this in the next chapter.) Of the sixteen hours you have remaining, about half of them are spent at work, assuming a least an eight-hour work day. Many people add additional work hours to their coveted weekends by checking email, finishing the report that's due Monday morning, obsessing over what transpired during the previous week, or planning/

worrying about the upcoming one. What we do with 50% of our lives is important, and it merits our full attention.

Optimize your workspace by cleaning up the messes, literally and figuratively. When you do so, you will be establishing yourself as a consummate pro upon whom others can rely to get the job done, each time.

CLUTTER-FREE WORKSPACE

It always puzzles me how people can say they work *better* in chaos. Frankly, I don't believe it. My theory is that many people who profess the power of clutter have numbed themselves to the agitation it causes and are so daunted by the specter of cleaning, organizing, and maintaining their workspaces that they justify the mess.

Clutter does *not* equal creativity.

Even if Feng Shui strikes you as a little too ethereal, there is a tangible loss of productivity when you waste time trying to find that file you "just know is around here somewhere …"

It also reflects poorly on you when someone observes the chaos. Your supervisors, colleagues, and customers are making opinions about you based not only on the work you do, but also on how you present yourself and how you treat your workspace. When was the last time the most disorganized, messy, unkempt person in your organization got a promotion? If you are a hot mess, people will quietly question your commitment, if not competence. "If Joe treats his space so shabbily, how can I expect him to have his act together on anything I would ask him to do?"

Maybe your clutter isn't in the physical space but rather the electronic one. Can you find files easily, or are you constantly hunting and pecking for that second version of the Board of Directors PowerPoint presentation you thought you put in the "BOD" folder? Are you constantly opening and closing files because you forgot what you named the document you need right now? Are your emails so out of control that you can't see daylight?

Make an honest assessment of your electronic and physical space the next time you go to work, and see what you can do to remove the clutter to create a pleasant command center for your innovative and creative juices to flow.

Don't let pieces of paper or files block your jam!

We deserve to enjoy our time at work as much as possible. We can impact the enjoyment and efficiency of our workspace by making a few simple modifications:

- If you have an office, use a few lamps instead of relying on fluorescent overhead lighting.

- Have healthy plants nearby.

- Play soft background music that makes you happy without distracting you.

- Frame awards, other commendations, testimonial letters from customers, and any other reminders of you and your company's awesomeness.

- Display current photos of your kids, both the two-legged and the four-legged kinds.

Even if you can't have (or don't want) a candle burning, aromatherapy wafting, or spa music playing, you still can invest a few minutes every single week in tidying up your space—tossing anything that is obsolete, taking your dirties to the breakroom (and *washing* them instead of leaving them for someone else to do), cleaning and wiping off your desk surface, and getting things prepped for next week. That will afford you the opportunity to have a stressless weekend and kick off the work week with enthusiasm!

SUITCASE GAME

Do you or your partner frequently travel either for business or pleasure? Is your open suitcase a constant fixture in the bedroom, often in the middle stages of half-packed, half-unpacked? Does it subtly remind you/judge you that your choice of employment keeps you away from home more than you or your family want it to?

As a professional speaker who is on the road as part of my livelihood, I found myself in that same situation. My suitcase was a symbol of where I was heading to or just arriving from. I experienced a quiet but persistent level of agitation every time my suitcase was out. Instead of ignoring my feelings, I decided to make it a game, so I could remain fully present while at home.

Every time I return from a trip of any kind—business or plea-sure—the *very* first thing I do upon arriving home (okay, maybe not the very first thing; that usually involves a trip to the loo) is to completely unpack my suitcase and put it back into the closet. Yes, even on red-eye days when all I want to do is crawl into my comfy bed and snuggle in my familiar sheets. I force myself to zip open the case, put my clothes in the laundry or back in the closet, re-stow bathroom stuff, and tuck my shoes back in the organizer.

You can also streamline the process by keeping an extra set of toiletries in a carry-on bag. That is one less thing you need to remember to pack.

I usually play some mid-tempo music and maybe make myself a Vitamin-C fizzy drink to keep my energy up for the exercise. (The Vitamin-C drink is always a good beverage to keep the immune system strong.) Before I know it, the process is complete, and I tuck my purple carry-on back in the front closet where it waits for its next mission.

Making a game of how fast you can unpack your suitcase—or put away your demonstration samples, or file your expenses, or anything else that ends a long work day—will help you cut the cord of that part of your journey, allowing you to fully arrive back at home, even if it's just for a little while. You deserve a day to be fully present in your home (and so do your loved ones!), not being reminded of all you have left to do.

After your next business trip, unpack with gusto! It will be the perfect way to start a wonderful day.

COACHING THROUGH CONFLICT

Up to this point I have focused on physical messes and objects. Mindful performance is also affected by messes within the office—messes created by performance issues and conflicts. Performance plummets when there is an unresolved conflict lurking in the hallways of your office. If you find yourself needing to coach an employee through a messy—even a quietly messy—performance or behavioral issue, use the recipe below to move through it cleanly, quickly, and amicably.

1. Ask the people with whom you have a conflict if you can briefly meet with them sometime soon to discuss your issue. Keep it general in scope, e.g. working better together, improving your relationship, communicating more effectively, balancing workloads, etc. Suggest a neutral location where you will not be disturbed. Nail down a time convenient for both of you that is not when anyone's energy may be compromised, such as at the end of the day or after a long work week. The person will likely ask what it is about and potentially be triggered or defensive. Reassure that it is not horrible and that you prefer to address it during your meeting. If possible, request this meeting be conducted in person versus on the phone. You do not want critical components of tone and facial expression to be lost since this is a vulnerable time in your relationship. Having this conversation face-to-face is ideal.

2. If you have a day's notice to prepare, make sure you get a good night's sleep (see the next chapter for tips on how to do that). On the day of your conversation, wear something comfortable and empowering but not intimidating. You don't want to be distracted by how you look or feel; you want to be fully present with the person in front of you instead of worrying if that shirt makes you look goofy.

3. Once you arrive at the meeting, make sure you are nonverbally communicating that you are open and receptive. Smile, shake the person's hand, maintain eye contact and set up the environment to be comfortable. Make small talk to diffuse the tension. Maybe even make a light, self-deprecating joke to add some humor.

4. Start by thanking the person for making a positive contribution to the organization or your life. Show appreciation. This will further dissipate and open communication.

5. Apologize. Be specific about how you have contributed to the problem you want to discuss. ("I apologize for not providing better training or constructive criticism in a timely fashion", "I apologize for not being more available to address your concerns before they became a problem", or "I apologize for not being clearer in my expectations and how I can help you be successful.") Be courageous. Be honest. Be humble. Your team member will emulate what you model. A sincere apology disarms even the most defensive person.

Take responsibility for your role in the conflict.

6. Directly address your areas of concern using facts instead of conjecture. ("On three separate occasions, you have arrived late for work.") Don't sound judgmental. Rather describe how the behavior is not congruent with the role or expectations. ("All customer service reps need to be ready to take calls by 9:00 a.m. for the organization to appropriately handle our customers' issues.") Avoid using words such as "always" or "never", seeing if you can say the word "you" as little as possible.

7. Be clear about what your expectations are and offer to help the person be more successful in moving forward. **Express your conviction that the person has the ability to work with you to reach a positive result.** Not only should you say this with your words, but with your eyes and your nonverbal communication. If you are not authentically approaching this behavior with a nonjudgmental attitude, the person will know it and shut down.

8. Ask for agreement on the course of action you will both take to rectify the situation. Assign a follow-up date to check in, and put it in your calendar immediately. No matter how or *if* the person changes, make sure you follow through. Share your observations and ask about the person's assessment of progress. Elicit feedback and ask how you can be even more helpful in his or her growth and development.

9. Thank the person for being open to receiving feedback that will help drive success. Leave the conversation on a friendly, positive note.

10. Document it all, just in case you need it later.

By taking these coaching steps in a purposeful way, you can take what was once a thorny issue and transform it into a powerful growth opportunity for you as a leader and your team member as a valued contributor.

You can also perform these steps for any peer-level conflict. Remember to solicit feedback on mistakes you might have made and what you can do to better align the relationship.

Conflict resolution is a two-way street. Don't shy away from it. Embrace it.

Leverage it to achieve greater results. By learning how to respectfully have difficult conversations, you will be armed with a powerful strategy that will remove barriers to your success, both at work and personally.

ALL DAY

....

When we become more mindful of our physical space, we establish small but powerful practices which reduce the negative stressors that keep us from being fully present and balanced.

BIG CLEANS

No matter how diligent you are about trying to stay on top of your physical space, the amount of input you are absorbing daily is likely larger than your output. You'll never, ever have a perfectly clean desk with nothing on it, patiently waiting for you to add some work to it whenever you get around to it. (If you do have a job like that, I would gently invite you to look at why you aren't challenging yourself more. It's okay to have more to do than time to do it; it's natural.) The same is true for our space at home. Closets explode with clothes. Garages get junky and jam-packed. Books and magazines multiply.

Because the inflow is inherently greater than the outflow, you would be wise to schedule Big Cleans on a regular basis. These are not windows of time where you will multi-task, cleaning up here and there while you do other activities. That doesn't work for Big Cleans. You don't clean out a filing cabinet while also painting a room, because a Big Clean requires more mental focus and physical energy than your typical day. You will work harder than you normally do during Big Cleans. Expect it. Don't make the process more laborious than it already is by throwing in other tasks that you'll do *while* you are trying to focus on that. Instead, just carve out the time, turn the phone off, shut down email, and put some music on. Dive in, touch a piece of paper, object, or computer file only once, and make a firm executive decision whether to give away (delegate), throw away (delete), or keep (do).

Give away/Throw Away/Keep: Those are the only things to focus on when you do a Big Clean.

Don't be tempted to chase after or execute any of the hidden nasties you might discover during your Big Clean. Just place it on the Keep pile (or the Keep folder) and move on. Your goal is to sort through the crap as quickly as possible, separating high-value items from the noise.

Once the Big Clean sorting exercise is complete, you can then turn your attention to the Throw Away pile. Shred away! There is absolutely no reason to keep items hanging around if no action is going to be taken or it no longer serves a meaningful purpose to you. If you *really* need to track down the four-inch, three-ring binder containing the TPS Report from August 2013, I'm sure someone else in the organization will be happy to oblige.

Next, attack the Give Away stuff with relentless abandon—get all of it off your plate! If you are doing a Digital Big Clean of your inbox, create a Give Away folder that houses all your delegated or forwardable items in one area. Once you are ready to clean out that folder, forward your email to each recipient, politely informing them of the change in ownership. Better yet, pick up the phone to alert them and offer your assistance if needed. Don't just throw it over to them without a proper introduction to the material.

After attacking your Throw Away and Give Away piles, you'll feel so light and liberated that your increased energy will help you dive into your Keep pile. Calendarize when you will accomplish each item and gather anything you'll need to complete each task.

NEED VS. WANT

The sorting process of Give Away/Throw Away/Keep is a highly effective practice that helps streamline our workspace, allowing us to keep our eyes only on those things that are relevant to our current work. That same categorization process works for everything we touch, whether we are at work, at home, in the car, on vacation, or wherever our feet are planted. However, it is often harder to do when the objects we are giving away or throwing away have personal, sentimental value or (potentially) high monetary worth. We are trained to hold on to possessions "just in case" we might need them someday.

Many of us grew up with parents or grandparents who lived through the Great Depression. (This is also an issue for many people who are immigrants from third world countries.) Throwing anything away was akin to a crime, committed by only the most selfish, reckless, and inconsiderate of us. My 95-year-old grandma washed out bread bags so she could reuse them repeatedly. The squirrel-away approach to physical objects was appropriate when there was a genuine and dire lack of basic resources to survive. However, that approach no longer ultimately serves us.

Why? Because we have *a lot* more stuff now, most of which we don't really need or want. I've gotten bags filled with trinkets at trade shows that will see the garbage can far sooner than they will see the light of day. From a business perspective, this is a colossal waste of money. Someone paid for the giveaways that end up in the trash. (One can, in fact, have too many koozies.) Consumption of anything we desire is a one-click purchase away, and it will be delivered to our door. What do we do with all that junk? Tuck it in drawers, corners, closets, garages, basements, and storage units—only to revisit it when moving from one home to another (or when our children go through it after we die.)

We can chip away at our tendency for overconsumption by being mindful. Before you plunk down your credit card for something shiny and new, I invite you to take a few deep breaths and ask yourself a key question: "Other than receiving an initial hit of dopamine, will this purchase ultimately serve me over time?" Or to make it simpler, ask yourself ...

"Do I really need this, or do I only want it?"

If you decide you don't really need a new set of golf clubs or another formal dress but really, really *want* it, then purchase it mindfully. Create the gap between stimulus and response to make a clear-headed decision in your long-term best interest. Understand the monetary impact. Identify its purposeful place in your home. Where will it reside? Sometimes taking a few conscious breaths and asking the Need versus Want question will be just the thing that will pop you out of the acquisition-dopamine loop.

You could even consider visualizing yourself using it, imagining how much fun it would be, how envied you may be by your colleagues, and any other superficial benefits you might experience. If you still feel like you absolutely, positively *must* have it, are there other, less expensive options you could purchase that would generate the same feeling? (I'm a huge fan of consignment shops! Reuse and recycle wherever possible.) Remember, most of us buy unnecessary items because they serve emotional needs. Chase after what needs they fill and see how you can generate those same feelings without having to waste your resources.

If you decide to make the purchase anyway, that's perfectly fine! However, to remain in balance with your space, consider swapping instead of just adding. As soon as you go home with your new goodie, immediately identify one item that is equivalent in function or size and remove it from your home. Put the item in your vehicle with a pledge that you'll gift your possession to a person you know who needs it, a business that will give you money for it, or a charitable organization that will repurpose it. Do this within a committed timeframe—Who's Going to do What by When.

Of all the Big Cleans I have done in my closet, I can recall exactly *one time* I wanted an item I had given away. At first, I was ticked off, but then I realized two things: 1) having only one incident with literally hundreds of giveaways over two decades is a pretty darned good ratio, and 2) I get to buy a brand new (or new-to-me) item to replace it!

SUPERSTRATEGY:
OWN YOUR MESSES

Now you know about the energy of space and how it impacts how we live and work. You know how messes in the workplace and at home negatively impact our performance, our mood, our relationships, and our success. Now it's time to deal with other kinds of messes. Messier messes. Messes that aren't as easy as wiping off the counter or sorting piles into Give Away/Throw Away/Keep.

One of the most life-changing habits you can establish on a personal and a professional level is to own your messes.

When you screw up, own it.

Declare to all those who are impacted by your mess that you are responsible for it and apologize. Get comfortable with saying, "I apologize". (I prefer "I apologize" over "I'm sorry", the latter having, to my ears, a subtle tone of childishness.) When we strengthen our confidence and get centered in our power, apologizing for our mistakes can be extremely liberating, which allows us to move quickly through conflict and into highly-effective, collaborative relationships.

Many of us learned as children that we only apologized after we were caught being "bad". As such, we grew up with an aversion to openly and courageously owning our missteps. When we aren't fully confident in our roles at work (or the numbers we are generating as sales professionals, or the stability of our relationships with our loved ones), we often try to hide our imperfections. Instead, we try to highlight only those examples where we look, sound, and act flawless. We try to put our best foot forward every time, avoiding the mistake monster with all our might. (Remember what happened to Tom Cruise in "Jerry Maguire" when he tried to own his mistakes! He got swiftly canned for having the gall to suggest greater client engagement.)

Ironically, this is a colossal error. The more we confidently own our messes, no matter how long ago or what the circumstances surrounding them are, the more powerful we are and more competent we appear to others. Fessing up to our roles in unpleasant situations without fear, hesitation, or excuses improves our reputation *if* we learn from the mistakes and make course corrections to ensure they don't happen again. Failures are the building blocks to success, so don't shy away from them. **Embrace the Oops!** Step firmly into the mistake, own it, and make a commitment that it will not be repeated.

If you want to improve your profitability, productivity, and purpose, I invite you to ask yourself some tough questions: Does your space and the objects in it—your home, your car, your office, your appearance, your communications—reflect you as a talented, reliable, well-liked, appreciative, and trusted partner? Are your personal and professional relationships healthy, your performance expectations clear, and your physical space organized and clean, or do they require some sprucing up? Are you sending the wrong message because you could be more mindful about your messes?

SELF-REFLECTION: MESSES

What are your strengths in this focus area?

_____

_____

_____

_____

What are your opportunities for growth?

_____

_____

_____

_____

What specific life experiences came up for you as you read through this chapter? What was the impact to you personally and professionally?

_____

_____

_____

_____

How would improving your activity and awareness in this focus area help you reach your goals?

_____

_____

_____

_____

What are the strategies that resonated with you the most?

- **Purposeful Places**
- **Fix-it List**
- **Home Spa Retreat**
- **Clutter-free Workspace**
- **Suitcase Game**
- **Big Cleans**
- **Need vs. Want**
- **Coaching Through Conflict**
- **Own Your Messes (SuperStrategy)**

What is one action you will take to increase your performance in this area, and by when will you do it?

_____

_____

_____

_____

CHAPTER 11

MEALS & ZZZZS

....

By this point we have seen the direct correlation between the inputs we absorb and what we send out into the world. Whether we want to look at them or not ...

two of the most critical factors that impact our performance are nutrition and sleep.

Conversely, if we ignore our bodies and their relationship to food and rest, we starve ourselves of the essential life force that propels us to be as productive as possible. According to a 2011 study in the *Journal of Sleep*, lack of sleep is costing U.S. companies a whopping $63 billion in lost productivity.[13] The Centers for Disease Control and Prevention describe the medical costs of obesity alone to be $147 billion annually in 2008 dollars.[14] Clearly, there is a need to be mindful of these two critical life factors, so we may be able to have the energy and vitality needed to be intentional in our success.

AT HOME

How we feed ourselves and promote healthy sleep are foundational to our mindful performance practice. Here are a few strategies to help you make better decisions so you can reap bigger rewards.

PROJECT DINNER

When I was in senior management of marketing and product development for a large telecommunications firm, my team was responsible for managing multi-million-dollar technology projects for global call centers. One of the most important aspects of successful project management is writing clear and complete requirements for the engineers and developers. My colleagues in Engineering would frequently remind me that if my team gave them weak product descriptions, then the product delivered would turn out weak. Conversely, if we wrote great specifications, the result would be great. Whenever we were in design sessions together, Engineering would tell those of us in Marketing to remember GIGO. In software development parlance, GIGO stood for "Garbage In, Garbage Out". It reinforced the importance of quality planning on the front end and how it impacts the result.

This handy memory device reminds us that whatever we take into our bodies (food, drink, media, conversations, air quality) has a direct correlation to our output.

If you are creating a stronger, more harmonious relationship with your physical body, ask yourself if what you take in is the highest quality fuel. Maybe the inputs (sugar, fatty foods, dairy, simple carbs) are contributing to some of the ailments you may be experiencing. If so, you may benefit from bringing some project management methods to your dining room table.

One of the ways you can do that is to treat feeding yourself and your family like a project. It requires a defined plan, buy-in from key stakeholders, sufficient resources, and action items with owners (preferably assigned to everyone in the home). When you execute Project Dinner—knowing what you are going to make, acquiring all ingredients, and assigning owners to tasks—you will be in right relation with food. A project doesn't need to be complicated. Use kitchen tools and appliances to make it fast and easy. However, keep a steady eye on GIGO, ensuring that your edible project has the best possible requirements from which to draw.

Look at the food in the breakroom and on your desk. Are you snacking on candy all day? Are you munching on donuts? What healthy food swaps can you make?

NIGHTTIME ROUTINE

The National Sleep Foundation suggests that bedtime rituals and schedules are key to promoting a healthy night's sleep. You will sleep more soundly if you create a nighttime ritual that allows you to slowly wind down after a long, stressful day.

Here are some strategies you may want to add to your nightly routine:

- Take a hot shower or a warm bath with essential oils and Epsom salts (don't forget the music and candles if you are a bath-freak like me!)

- Tidy up your bedroom, removing any piles of clothes or other displaced items that may be contributing to the restless energy that clutter brings.

- Write in your journal or jot down your Top 3 Will Do's for the following day.

- Listen to soothing music that lulls you to a calmer state.

- Read a few pages of a book that is soul-feeding or inspiring.

- Stretch on a yoga mat to twist and fold the day's stress away.

- Try slow breathing. Inhale to the count of five, hold your breath for a count of five, and exhale to a count of five. Gradually increase the number of seconds you spend in each part of the breathing cycle.

Creating time for these sleep-promoting activities may cut into your media time or other leisure activities, but it is worth it. Stick to a standard bedtime as much as possible so you can be refreshed and restored in the morning. By creating nighttime rituals, you will establish healthy habits that will have a huge, long-term impact on your health, vitality, and performance.

BEDSIDE NOTES

Many of us have found ourselves completely wiped out at the end of a long work day, only to find that we can't seem to fall asleep once we are in bed. We toss and turn, attempting to find a comfortable position to soothe our weary bodies. When we finally settle our bodies down, our minds take over to run the party. We vainly try to fight off the onslaught of random thoughts swirling in our heads: "What is on my plate tomorrow?", "How can I help my child?", "I need to remember to make that doctor's appointment!", or "What's the name of that song I heard on the radio?" Shutting down our mental chatter is key to getting a full night's sleep, at least until we need to get up for that middle-of-the-night bathroom visit.

Here's a strategy you can use to help clear out those pesky thoughts. Have a small notebook and pen on your nightstand to capture any stream of consciousness thoughts that endlessly knock around your brain. Oftentimes we stay awake because we are forcing ourselves to remember something important (or something we think is) instead of just taking the initiative to write it down and forget about it.

By directly addressing your thoughts, you can get the ZZZZs you need to wake up feeling refreshed, restored, and raring to go for the day. I like to think of my notebook as a siphon that allows me to drain my brain of excess information that isn't serving me at bedtime. During your morning routine you can review last night's entry and see if there are, in fact, items you need to act on. If so, get your calendar out and schedule them. Chances are, however, that much of what you were noodling at night really isn't that important once it sees the light of day.

You can also use your bedside notebook to write down a pressing question or problem you have been wrestling with, either at work or at home. What issue is dogging you that you can't seem to address? Some of your questions may be: "How can I connect to my elusive prospect?", "What am I missing in my leadership style that is causing my team to disengage?", "What would be the most important action I could take that would help me to be more balanced and healthy?", or "How can I create better communication with my partner, child, or friend?" Let those questions be the last things you read before you go to sleep.

Oftentimes our unconscious minds will tackle these problems while we sleep. Solutions may come in the form of a dream or an a-ha insight immediately upon waking. Other times it may show itself in the form of gentle Cosmic Noogies that point you to the answer. The answers may not show themselves right away, but if you keep at it, your mind training will eventually either show you the answer or give you guidance as to how to graciously accept the status quo without further emotional upset. By clarifying exactly what you want answers to, you are giving your mind an assignment that it will complete (and maybe then some). When you get intentional about utilizing your unconscious mind for support, you will be surprised at the amount of insight and inspiration it will deliver for you.

AT WORK

Just because you aren't at home or in the kitchen doesn't mean you shouldn't prioritize Meals and ZZZZs at work too. We spend approximately half of our conscious waking lives at work, so we would be wise to watch how we are fueling ourselves and restoring our energy.

FOR THE LOVE OF LUNCH

When I work with clients on mindful culture consulting and leadership training, I observe how they are taking care of themselves ... or not. So many workers bounce back and forth from being overwhelmed to being disengaged, and it becomes apparent in how they treat themselves.

There is a growing number of smart leaders who promote healthy self-care, knowing it improves employee engagement and performance. However, there are still lots of others who have fostered unhealthy cultures where team members don't invest in taking care of themselves for fear that they will be seen as slackers or not as committed to the cause as their co-workers. Nowhere is this more present than the humble lunch hour.

How many times have you scarfed down lunch at your desk or skipped it altogether because you are "too busy?" When you do eat lunch, what do you choose? Do you have fast food, vending machine selections, or donuts from the break room? We have allowed lunch to be relegated to an afterthought instead of giving it the love it deserves.

Consider reorienting yourself to the importance of lunch. It is a critical meal to refuel your body for the second half of your work day—the half that may be even more productive than the morning. It is also time for you to step away from the craziness and digital devices that keep you spinning at a higher frequency. When mindfully prepared, you can also use it to keep those nasty extra pounds at bay because you are eating healthier, more filling foods that will keep you from the 3:00 p.m. sugar crash so many of us suffer from.

Don't let lunch be an undervalued task you rush through.

Plan for it ahead of time to set yourself up for success. Make your lunch either the night before or in the morning, making sure you wake up early enough to pack your lunchbox without having to be stressed out. Choose plenty of foods that will keep your energy high; protein, fruits, vegetables, and nuts are great solutions. Get those little plastic containers so you can have a variety of options. Pack two cloth napkins so you can use one and have the other as a placemat. Of course, always have a sturdy water bottle available so you can hydrate yourself instead of loading up on caffeine or sugar.

If you are going out to eat because it is necessary (not because you failed to plan), then treat it as if you were preparing your own lunch. Don't let the delectable offerings sway you from making good choices about your health. If you know you have a challenging time resisting the bread basket or the dessert tray, drink extra water to fill yourself up immediately before going out. If you find yourself ordering something that isn't quite as nutritionally balanced as you would like, then immediately ask the server for a to-go box so you can put half of it away as soon as your meal is served. If the food is in front of you, you will eat it, sometimes completely without awareness. However, if you put it in the to-go box right away, you are far less likely to break into the Styrofoam and dig into that food.

Not only will your colleagues, customers, and supervisor notice your mindful eating, they will make extrapolations about your competency as a professional. If you eat in a conscious way, then you are likely to work consciously as well. You'll be respected and envied while seeing the benefits inside and out from the choices you have made. Lunch deserves love, and it will love you in return.

BODY BALANCE SHEET

All this healthy talk is well and good, but what about when the Reese's Peanut Butter Cups in the cafeteria are calling to you? We all have those moments where chocolate is a must-have. What can you do to make it a mindful selection?

One strategy to help you see the results of your choices is to consider your Body Balance Sheet. Assets and liabilities impact our physical health just like they impact the financial health of our organizations. It's an asset to our well-being when we make healthy food choices, when we move, and when we have calming, meditative moments. We incur liabilities the longer we eat junk food, sit on our chairs, and stew about the latest stressor. We are adding and subtracting from our Body Balance Sheet every single day—during client dinners, at the airport, when we go for brunch, all the time. When we add a large amount of food to our liabilities column, what can we add in the asset column to balance it out?

It's just a simple matter of math. Make additional contributions in the movement department if you are going to add to your caloric intake. If you choose to eat those delicious chocolate/peanut butter cups of heaven, then add 210 calories worth of movement. Park your car as far away as you can. Walk up and down the stairs several times. Take the scenic route to the conference room. Do some stretches. Lift a box of paper from the storage closet to the copier.

Move, move, move.

Meals and movement are directly correlated to your health, happiness, and success.

MID-DAY SHUT-EYE

For years my mother used to take a daily nap in the middle of her workday. She called it her "half-hour power". Some forward-thinking companies have seen the light when it comes to the power of sleep. Productivity Guru Michael Hyatt has long been a strong advocate for the daily snooze. Nap stations are popping up at airports, and sleep pods are being used in companies like Google, Cisco, and even PricewaterhouseCoopers! If you are lucky enough to have access to these types of facilities and policies, good for you! You work for an amazing company. If not, you can still find a few minutes every day to close your eyes for a little bit and reset your system.

During your lunch break, consider taking the second half as naptime. Taking just a 20-minute catnap can be all you need to rev up your engine. If you have a private office, bring a small pillow upon which to rest your head. If you don't, you can use your car and get a neck pillow to give yourself some support. You may even want to create a little note that says, "I'm Fine; Just Catnapping!" and place on the window so onlookers don't start worrying about you. (Make sure you lock your doors for safety's sake.)

Even if you can't steal away for 20 minutes to take a formal nap, consider taking an extra-long break where you can close your eyes for a bit and just breathe. This can be done in an empty conference room, a breakroom, or even a bathroom stall! Just close your eyes for a bit and do some conscious breathing exercises. You will feel refreshed after having stepped away from the screens if only for a few precious minutes.

A word of caution: It is *imperative* that your supervisor and company are overtly supportive of Mid-day Shut-eyes, otherwise you run the risk of experiencing negative consequences (including termination). In addition, if you are not able to limit the duration of your naps and can't get right back into focused work mode, this strategy is not for you. Only you know if this performance-enhancing technique is right for your work situation.

ALL DAY

Below are some helpful concepts and strategies you can utilize at any time to maintain a healthy relationship with food and sleep, so you can have consistent, high-octane energy throughout the entire day … and your life.

EARTH-BASED EATING

"An apple a day keeps the doctor away." And the energy high. And the digestion functioning as designed. And the weight off.

If I eat an apple every day, I feel better. Period. I eat less junk. My digestive system works better. I have more clarity. My energy is higher. That's what earth-based eating does for us.

Choose foods that are as close to the earth as possible.

If it walked on the land, swam in the ocean, grew in the ground, or blossomed on a tree, chances are it is wicked good for you. Nature provides us with a cornucopia of choices, and there are natural foods out there to suit every taste. You may need to invest additional time in learning about proper preparation and seasoning to make earth-based foods taste yummy, but it is well worth the time.

Become mindful of the number of boxes, bottles, and bags you are using at mealtime. They usually indicate a higher level of processing, which brings with it higher sodium levels, massive sugar, and other unknown chemicals which can wreak havoc on our energy levels and waistlines. Pay attention to what is in your recycling bin before you take it to the curb. What evidence is there of choices that were far away from nature's bounty? Can you replace one of those selections with a healthier choice next time? Don't judge yourself for past poor choices. Just learn from them and move on. Leave the judgment for the courts, not your kitchen.

The more frequently we eat filling, earth-based foods, the less likely we'll choose something naughty. And the older we get, the less forgiving our bodies are to bad choices. It's incredibly easy to gain weight and a lot harder to lose it. I can simply think about a chocolate éclair and add five pounds to my butt. After losing 50 pounds and keeping it off for several years, I'd rather just focus my efforts on maintaining instead of losing. It's a heckuva lot easier.

What can you do to add more whole foods to your diet? How can you prepare yourself to combat the mid-afternoon hangries? What one food choice can you make that will supercharge your energy like the apple does for me? Make eating those types of food a habit. Your energy will skyrocket.

SUPERSTRATEGY:
ANALOG HOURS

I'm old enough to remember things like rotary phones. Card catalogs. Record stores. These were ways we entertained ourselves back in the stone age. If we wanted to learn about a subject, we went to the library to look it up courtesy of Dewey and his decimal system. We used actual shopping carts to shop. We used our fingers to write on paper, not our thumbs to press screens. We bought entire albums and listened to every track, studying the liner notes for hours. We used ginormous paper maps to navigate our journeys instead of letting Siri tell us where to go. (Sometimes when Siri steers me in the wrong direction, I want to tell her where to go.) This analog living kept our brains and bodies active.

Unfortunately, digital living has largely taken over and with it, some negative effects in many areas of our lives, not the least of which is the quality of our sleep. What is your brain taking in right before you drift off to sleep? Are you watching shows about war, crime, or the zombie apocalypse, complete with imagery that shows unimaginable terror and violence? While your conscious brain knows that these unspeakable acts aren't happening to you, other parts of your brain don't know the difference. They are still making imprints in your neural network which find their way into your subconscious mind, thus altering and damaging an otherwise peaceful night's sleep. A study done in the journal *Dreaming* showed that those who watched violent images immediately before going to sleep were 13 times more likely to have violent dreams than those who did not.

Maybe you aren't watching any shows before bed but merely surfing news sites and social media. Are you reading about the latest political scandal? The last horrific attack on innocent people? The endless complaining from Facebook spewers about how life isn't the way they want it? When we make our screens the last thing we touch, we stay awake longer than our bodies want us to. Our eyes hurt from the glow. We are feeding ourselves negative messaging that robs us of precious quality quiet time we could be using to feed our spirits, not sapping us of it.

Carve out analog hours before going to bed and upon waking to read a book instead of surfing your device. Read something empowering, illuminating, educational, or inspirational. Get a book lamp so you can read in comfort without disrupting your partner. Feel the pages on your fingertips.

Take your time with your book. Enjoy it. Bask in the quiet.

Let the words envelope you, knowing you are intentionally feeding your subconscious mind with good mental fuel that will help you get a better night's sleep … and supercharge your performance.

PRO-ACTIVE PRODUCTIVITY

Eating healthfully and getting ample sleep are easy things to say, and we all know we need to do them. But accomplishing those simple-but-oh-so-challenging goals can be much more difficult. Many of us have a complicated relationship with food, which impacts our ability to make good choices on a consistent basis. Even when we think we are making good choices, our bodies may not agree. Similarly, we may have tried every single strategy listed in this book but still struggle.

As I have mentioned several times throughout "Mindful Performance," sometimes we reach a point in our journeys where we simply can't do it on our own. We need the help of a trusted, talented professional to see the results we want. You may want to get some guidance from a food counselor or personal trainer for nutritional challenges. Reach out to a professional who specializes in the area of nutrition if you don't know what your body really needs to function optimally. Our bodies change over time, and it's quite possible that what once worked for you to maintain a healthy body isn't what you need now.

Consider going to a sleep specialist if you are still having difficulty getting enough sleep despite trying all the strategies I've shared. Participate in a sleep study to see what your sleep patterns really are. You may find that you would benefit from getting a CPAP machine or other sleep therapy devices.

An essential aspect to executing any of the strategies in *Mindful Performance* is to get the support you need as quickly as possible.

224

Don't do it alone.

Sometimes the very ingredient missing from our full activation is a professional who can walk us through the confusion, emotional challenge, and need for accountability.

When we bring greater awareness and mindful choices to the fuel we take in and the restoration we need, we show up more fully in every exchange, have more energy to expend, and manage our emotions in a more balanced fashion.

When our tanks are full, and our bodies are in optimal condition, there is simply no limit to what we can accomplish!

SELF-REFLECTION:
MEALS & ZZZZs

What are your strengths in this focus area?

_____

_____

_____

_____

What are your opportunities for growth?

_____

_____

_____

_____

What specific life experiences came up for you as you read through this chapter? What was the impact to you personally and professionally?

_____

_____

_____

_____

How would improving your activity and awareness in this focus area help you reach your goals?

_____

_____

_____

_____

What are the strategies that resonated with you the most?

- **Project Dinner**
- **Nighttime Routine**
- **Bedside Notes**
- **For the Love of Lunch**
- **Body Balance Sheet**
- **Mid-day Shut-eye**
- **Earth-based Eating**
- **Analog Hours (SuperStrategy)**
- **Pro-active Productivity**

What is one action you will take to increase your performance in this area, and by when will you do it?

_____

_____

_____

_____

CHAPTER 12

EMBODYING THE MODEL

....

You did it! You have discovered all the rich secrets and powerful strategies of "Mindful Performance" designed to help you establish a robust, multi-layered mindfulness practice that will dramatically transform your life inside and out. You will establish new habits and neural patterns. You will release old programs and harmful choices that have held you back. Before you know it, you've accomplished what you set out to do: you will powerfully impact your profitability, productivity, and purpose.

Commit to assessing your current condition on a regular basis in order to continue to make progress on being more mindful at work, at home, and all day. Every month rate yourself on a scale of 1 to 10 in each area of the *Mindful Performance Model*. If you assess yourself at a level of 7 or less, revisit the corresponding chapter to brush up on a strategy, mindset, or tool that can improve your numbers. Cut yourself some slack when you trip up, and get back on track ASAP.

MINDFUL PERFORMANCE MODEL
MONTHLY SELF ASSESSMENT

On a scale of 1 to 10 (1 being the lowest and 10 being ideal), rate your level of mindfulness in each segment.

One of the most impactful actions you can take to embody the *Mindful Performance Model* is to make a commitment to surround yourself with other mindful people. They are easy to spot: they are those who are successful, healthy, and happy. They don't complain. They have rich, rewarding relationships. They command a great deal of respect from leaders in their industries. They make you happy when you are in their presence. Spend as much quality time with these rock stars as possible. Conversely, set boundaries and limit time spent with those who are disconnected and act unconsciously in the areas discussed in "Mindful Performance." You can recognize them easily too: they are the people who whine incessantly, never catch a break, have bodies and relationships that are falling apart, and spread negativity everywhere they go. You feel worse when you are around them. They act like poison to your creativity and growth. Stay away from them as much as humanly possible.

The 81 strategies in "Mindful Performance" are small choices relatively speaking, but they have an enormous impact when performed consistently over time. Small choices, significant impact. Day by day. Moment by moment.

You will build the life and career of your dreams, one mindful choice at a time.

Build on that momentum and start sharing your wisdom with others.

Thank you for reading this book, dear one. I know you had a choice to do something else – something easier and more comfortable. My life's work is dedicated to inspiring people just like you to reach higher, shine brighter, and live better. I am committed to helping you powerfully impact your profitability, productivity, and purpose. When you do so, you will be able to serve others in return. You'll make work more meaningful for your team. You'll come up with innovations that will solve some of our most pressing issues. You'll be better parents to your kids.

Now, go do great things with your newly unleashed energy. The world needs you.

MINDFUL
PERFORMANCE
MATRIX

....

Strategies, Mindsets, and Tools to Help You Powerfully Impact Your Profitability, Productivity, and Purpose

SuperStrategies in bold

MOVEMENT		
AT HOME	**AT WORK**	**ALL DAY**
• Move Right Away	• Rise at the Zeroes	• Joyful Movement
• Morning Momentum	• Smart Inefficiency	• Make a Date
• Movement Toolkit	• Squeeze and Release	• **Grounding Your Energy**

MEDITATIONS		
AT HOME	**AT WORK**	**ALL DAY**
• Start with the Breath	• Mental Defrag	• Body Scan
• Meditation-in-a-Minute	• Outcome Energization	• Emotional Audit
• MindPower Calisthenics	• Pre-performance Prep	• **Focus on the BMI**

MANIFESTATIONS		
AT HOME	**AT WORK**	**ALL DAY**
• **Statement of Intention**	• Resource Readiness	• See the Parking Spot
• Thought Energy	• Who's Going to Do What by When	• The Cosmic Noogie
• Deliberate Living	• Post-it Power	• **Gratitude Rant**

MEETINGS

AT HOME	AT WORK	ALL DAY
• House Meeting Logistics • Complete Conversations • Embracing Emotion	• Money Value of Time • Unified Arrival • Mindful Meeting Mastery	• Name-calling • **Story or Spreadsheet** • Person of Increase

MENTORS & MASTERMINDS

AT HOME	AT WORK	ALL DAY
• Go Forth and Delegate • Pick Your Victories • Specifics Over Silence	• Earn Before the Ask • Do What Your Mentors Say • Mastermind Mechanics	• **Gut-punch of Truth** • Personal Advisory Board • Game Footage

MESSAGES		
AT HOME	**AT WORK**	**ALL DAY**
• Polarity Potholes • I Over You • Yes, and	• Delightful Networking • Thought-full Emails • Spewer vs. Doer	• The Middle Way • Guerilla Positivity • **Two Words**

MEDIA		
AT HOME	**AT WORK**	**ALL DAY**
• Technology Medicine • Conscious Bingeing • Book Scanning	• Sanctioned Distractions • Money-making Media • Flying Free	• By the Numbers • Solo and Smartphone-free • **Media Fasts**

MESSES		
AT HOME	**AT WORK**	**ALL DAY**
• Purposeful Places • Fix-it List • Home Spa Retreat	• Clutter-free Workspace • Suitcase Game • Coaching Through Conflict	• Big Cleans • Need vs. Want • **Own Your Messes**

MEALS & ZZZZs		
AT HOME	**AT WORK**	**ALL DAY**
• Project Dinner • Nighttime Routine • Bedside Notes	• For the Love of Lunch • Body Balance Sheet • Mid-day Shut-eye	• Earth-based Eating • **Analog Hours** • Pro-active Productivity

HELPFUL RESOURCES

....

These books are excellent resources on mindfulness, levels of consciousness, and high-performance leadership.

Gelles, David, and Podehl, Nick. *Mindful Work: How Meditation is Changing Business from the Inside Out*

Newport, Cal. *Deep Work: Rules for Focused Success in a Distracted World*

Mumford, George. *The Mindful Athlete: Secrets to Pure Performance*

Dweck, Carole and Gavin, Marguerite. *Mindset: The New Psychology of Success*

Tenney, Matt, and Gard, Tim. *The Mindfulness Edge: How to Rewire Your Brain for Leadership and Personal Excellence Without Adding to Your Schedule*

Hill, Napeoleon. *Think and Grow Rich*

Tan, Chade-Meng, and Sullivan, Nick. *Search Inside Yourself: The Unexpected Path to Achieving Success, Happiness (and World Peace)*

Judith, Anodea. *Eastern Body, Western Mind: Psychology and the Chakra System as a Path to the Self; Creating on Purpose: The Spiritual Technology of Manifesting Through the Chakras*

Lohrenz, Carey. *Fearless Leadership: High-Performance Lessons from the Flight Deck*

Combs, Deirdre, and Fox, Matthew. *The Way of Conflict: Elemental Wisdom for Resolving Disputes and Transcending Differences*

Marturano, Janice. *Finding the Space to Lead: A Practical Guide to Mindful Leadership*

Gawain, Shakti. *Creative Visualization: Use the Power of Your Imagination to Create What You Want in Your Life*

NOTES

1 https://www.apa.org/news/press/releases/stress/2017/state-nation.pdf

2 https://www.stress.org/workplace-stress/

3 https://www.mindful.org/jon-kabat-zinn-defining-mindfulness/

4 https://news.aetna.com/2017/06/aetna-opens-first-mindfulness-center/

5 https://www.cdc.gov/healthcommunication/toolstemplates/entertain-mented/tips/PhysicalInactivity.html

6 http://journals.sagepub.com/doi/abs/10.1111/j.1467-9280.2008.02225.x

7 Gelles, David, Mindful Work: How Meditation is Changing Business from the Inside Out, Eamon Dolan/Mariner Books, 2016

8 Jackson, Phil, Eleven Rings, Penguin Books, 2014

9 https://www.tonyrobbins.com/documentary/

10 https://integraladvisors.com/wp-content/uploads/2013/02/State-Of-the-American-Manager.pdf

11 https://hbr.org/2018/01/why-people-really-quit-their-jobs

12 http://themindlab.co.uk/pr/did-you-know/

13 https://aasm.org/insomnia-costing-u-s-workforce-63-2-billion-a-year-in-lost-productivity-study-shows/

14 https://www.cdc.gov/obesity/adult/causes.html

ACKNOWLEDGEMENTS

....

I am so grateful for the many people in my life who have helped me bring this project to fruition. Without their friendship, love, counsel, and support, you would not be holding this book in your hands right now.

To Connie Podesta, my mentor and dear friend who showed me my true potential as a keynote speaker and gave me the roadmap to get there.

To Patricia Iyer who provided priceless edits and suggestions that took a good book and made it great.

To Kendra Cagle for designing the book so beautifully and thoughtfully.

To Jean McManis, my best friend, sister-from-another-mister, and recipient of my late-night phone calls who gives me constant encouragement when I feel like crumbling.

To Dawnna St. Louis, a speaking force of nature who helped me gain clarity on my expertise and how to create a thought leadership model to support it.

To Kristen Brown, Merit Gest, and Janel Anderson, three of my dear friends and accountability partners who were always available to provide feedback and encouragement during the messy creative process.

To all my colleagues in the National Speakers Association who have taught me so much about the craft of speaking and the importance of sharing our teachings in written form.

To my wonderful clients who have trusted in me to help them achieve greater mindful performance.

Finally, to Emma Rose, my incredible daughter and reason for being. Thank you for supporting me every mindful step of the way.

ABOUT THE AUTHOR

Theresa Rose is a smart, savvy, persuasive, business motivational speaker, award-winning author, former sales and marketing executive, and sought-after expert on leadership, sales, change, and communication. She is the Past President of the Minnesota Chapter of the National Speakers Association and a top five finalist in the "So You Think You Can Speak?" competition. Theresa taps into her depth and breadth of experience as an organizational leader, successful businesswoman, and whip-smart comedian to help organizations and their teams powerfully impact their profitability, productivity, and purpose. Theresa is the proud mom of her daughter Emma and enjoys living in the great state of Minnesota. You betcha.

For more information on Theresa's work
or to read additional articles, visit **TheresaRose.com.**

BOOK THERESA

....

If you are looking for an engaging speaker who can help your organization increase sales and revenue, develop stronger leaders, create better connections, and build healthier cultures, Theresa Rose is for you! She incorporates infectious comedy, audience interaction, relevant storytelling, and actionable content to create a one-of-a-kind experience for attendees. Theresa is an electrifying performer who delivers customized programs that are perfectly tied to organizational mission and event theme, and she leaves her audiences motivated, entertained, and armed with memorable key takeaways they can utilize long after the event is over. Her energizing presentations deliver the content, value, and ROI you need to make a lasting impact!

- Increase focus and reduce distraction so you can show up more powerfully and persuasively in every exchange.

- Cultivate rock-solid, long-term relationships with your customers and teams.

- Create mindful cultures that get your team to want to come to work every day ... and actually work.

- Dramatically increase your performance while creating greater levels of balance and personal satisfaction.

Email **Theresa@TheresaRose.com** to discuss your event and how you can partner with her to create a fabulous experience for your audience!